Holbeton, Devon

Bench-Ends in English Churches

BY

J. CHARLES COX, LL.D., F.S.A.

Author of "Churches of Derbyshire" (4 vols.), "Churches of Cambridgeshire,"
"Churches of Cornwall," "Churches of Cumberland and Westmorland,"
"Churches of the Isle of Wight," "Churches of Nottinghamshire," ",How
to Write the History of a Parish," "Churchwardens' Accounts," "Parish
Registers," "Church Furniture," "Royal Forests of England," "Sanctuaries,"
"Pulpits, Lecterns, and Organs," Etc.

WITH 164 ILLUSTRATIONS

HUMPHREY MILFORD

OXFORD UNIVERSITY PRESS

London, New York, Toronto, Melbourne, and Bombay

1916

PRINTED AT
THE DARIEN PRESS
EDINBURGH

PREFACE

IN visiting a vast number of the ancient parish churches throughout England and Wales during the past half century, hardly
anything, so far as their interior is concerned, has excited greater
interest or attention on the part of the writer than their seating,
more especially that of early or pre-Reformation days. The
exceptional skill of the old craftsmen, displaying rare artistic
power in the designing and executing of varied series of bench-
ends, was a subject of joy and admiration during a boyhood
and youth chiefly spent in Somersetshire and Devonshire, and
this feeling materially increased when I came to study the
bounteous stores of East Anglia in the 'sixties and 'seventies of
last century. Throughout a long life it has been my wish to
draw attention to the skilled carpentry of the mediæval period to
be found throughout the churches of all the shires, which, in the
case of seating, is so essentially English. Several most capable
writers and draughtsmen have of late years done abundant
justice to our rood-screens, which are still so numerous notwithstanding the havoc created by the crass ignorance or puritanical
Philistinism of would-be restorers; but no monograph has yet
been issued dealing with the subject of the seats from the
thirteenth century downwards. Mr Bond's most admirably
illustrated series of books on Church Art in England has at
last afforded me the long-desired opportunity, for which I am
grateful, of producing lists of examples covering the whole area.
They will probably be of use to students and architects as well
as to that portion of the reading public which is interested in
ecclesiology. The lists aim at completeness, but are quite sure
to fall short of perfection, arising from strict limits of space.
The very numerous examples mentioned, with very brief comments, in the following pages have all been personally examined,
with the exception of one or two in Lancashire and Herefordshire. The short chapter on galleries is from Mr Bond's pen.

J. C. C.

v

Mr Bond, the general editor of the series, is responsible for the selection, arrangement, and reproduction of the photographs. Modern work is represented only by two illustrations from Holbeton; fine examples at Wymondham abbey, the Leys school chapel at Cambridge and elsewhere, have had to be excluded for lack of space.

For permission to reproduce photographs, acknowledgments are due to Mr F. S. Aldridge, Dr F. J. Allen, Mr A. W. Anderson, Mr E. W. Andrew, Mr Thomas Baddeley, Miss F. Baquist, Mr H. Creighton Beckett, Mr L. Berry, Mr R. H. Brierley, Dr G. Granville Buckley, Mr T. Bundock, Dr P. B. Burroughs, Dr Oscar Clark, Mr T. Coysh, Mr F. H. Crossley, Mr W. Marriott Dodson, Mr J. Dowson, Mr G. C. Druce, Mr J. F. East, Mrs C. H. Eden, Mr G. J. Gillham, Mr T. M. Grose-Lloyd, Mr Everard L. Guilford, Mr Philip M. Johnston, Mr H. E. Illingworth, Mr W. Maitland, Rev. Walter Marshall, Mr James Norman, Mr C. F. Nunneley, Mr W. Page, Mr W. Percival-Wiseman, Miss E. K. Prideaux, Rev. G. W. Saunders, Rev. R. M. Serjeantson, Mr C. B. Shuttleworth, Rev. Frederick Sumner, Mr F. R. P. Sumner, Mr F. R. Taylor, Mr Henry Walker, Mr G. H. Widdows, Mr E. W. M. Wonnacott, and many others, whose photographs, for lack of space, it was not possible to reproduce, and to whom also acknowledgments are due. The photographs reproduced are distinguished by the initials of the owner of the photograph. The illustration on p. 109 is reproduced from Mr Bond's book on " Dedications." Lists of the chief works consulted are given on p. 191 ; other references will be found in footnotes to the text. An index to the illustrations and to the places mentioned in the text, and an index of persons and subjects, are given at the end of the volume; the former index has been prepaied by Dr Cox, the latter by Mr Bond.

F. B.

TABLE OF CONTENTS

BENCH-ENDS IN ENGLISH CHURCHES

PART I

CHAPTER I

Original Use, only Kneeling or Standing—The Eastern Churches—Stone Seats against Walls and round Piers—Wooden Seats—Exeter Synod of 1287—Thirteenth Century Seats—Later Fixed Seats—The Word "Pew"—Thame Parish Accounts—Excellency of Oak—Arrangement and Character of Fixed Seats—Great Variety of Bench-Ends— Passion Emblems — "Poppy - Heads" — Backless Benches — Lay Patrons and Official Claims to Chancel Seats.

IT would appear that the early custom of the whole Catholic Church, so far as the congregation was concerned, was to stand when not kneeling during Divine service. To this custom there can be no doubt that the Church of England conformed for several centuries. Sitting during worship was an almost unknown position, as it still is throughout all the Eastern Churches, whether Greek, Russian, Coptic, or Armenian. From the walls of the Greek churches, arms project to give some support to the standing worshippers who may need it, but the unaided erect posture in supplication to God is the traditional and accepted use throughout all the Churches of the East.[1]

[1] In this connection it should be remembered that sermons, covering an extended period of standing, are but exceptional incidents in the Greek Church. In the modern Greek churches of St Sophia, Bayswater, and of St Nicholas, Liverpool, a certain amount of seats are provided, out of concession to the English, but these are chiefly used by visitors. See Archdeacon Dowling's most interesting book on "Hellenism in England" (1915).

I

But in the course of time this aversion to seats in places of worship weakened in the Churches of the West, and more especially in England, where it eventually resulted, as we shall presently see, in the soul-stifling habit, even in pre-Reformation days, of class distinction, and the allotment and sale of seats in the House of God.

The early fabrics of English churches lacked all wooden fittings ; the altar was of stone, as also were the Mass seats on the south of the quire. As to the congregation, there were stone seats or bench-tables against the walls, which would suffice for the aged or infirm, whilst others in a like condition would be permitted to bring with them a mat or even a stool. These stone benches attached to the base of the walls are far more common than is usually supposed, while a great number have been cleared away when restoration brought about the renewal of the outer walls. Thus in Chaldon church, Surrey, a long, low stone seat ran along the wall of the south aisle until 1871, when it was "restored" away. The earliest of the churches of Cornwall seem always to have had these stone benches, as at St Perran-Zabuloe, where a stone seat 16 in. high and 14 in. broad runs all round the building, interrupted only by doorways and altar ; the same may be noted in the much later south transepts of both Minster and Tintagel.

Another effective and more unusual manner of providing structural sitting accommodation was to place stone seats round the piers of arcaded naves. This occurs with some frequency in Nottinghamshire, where the circular seats may be noted round the piers of Coddington, Kirton, Kneesall, Laxton, Lowdham, North Muskham, Norwell, South Scarle, Scarrington, Sutton Bonnington, South Wakeringham, and Warsop (7). Wall benches are also to be noted in this county (see Dr Cox's "Churches of Nottinghamshire," p. 12).

A list is subjoined of other counties besides Cornwall and Nottinghamshire, where we have personally observed the old stone seats, and we must have seen, during a long period of church hunting, at least as many more of which we took no written note. This list is set forth to help to disprove the current notion that these stone bench-tables are a great rarity. It is not unlikely that their existence in churches originated the proverb that—"The weakest goes to the wall."

Bedfordshire—Sundon, north and south aisles. *Cambridgeshire*—Sutton and Over, round church. *Cheshire*—Acton, all round church and chancel. *Cumberland*—March, round piers. *Derbyshire*—Norbury, each side of chancel. Weston-on-Trent,

Abbotsham, Devon

F. S.

north of north aisle and west of south aisle. *Kent*—Adisham, both sides of nave. Bapchild, round north chapel. Lydd, round piers. *Lincolnshire*—Bottesford, Caistor, and Claypole, all round piers. *Norfolk*—Hunstanton and Snettisham, round piers. Tunstead, both aisles. *Northamptonshire*—Cottesbroke and Ufford, round the aisles. Warmington, each side of chancel. *Oxfordshire*—Ipsden, north and west walls. *Rutland*—Tixover, each side of chancel. *Somersetshire*—Moulton, round piers. Priddy and North Petherton, south aisle. Brimpton, west end. *Sussex*—New Shoreham, aisles (7). *Warwickshire*—Stratford - on - Avon, round western piers. *Wiltshire*—Bishopstone, south and west walls of south transept. Bratton, round piers of central tower. *Yorkshire*—Hemingborough, south and west walls. Kirby Sigston, north aisle. Middleton, north and west walls. Patrington, round nave.

Church porches were usually provided with stone benches, which chiefly served for rest both before and after the services. A like use was made of the lowest step of the churchyard cross, particularly in Somersetshire, where they are numerous ; we have known the last century sextons of both Luccombe and Selworthy, in West Somerset, leave the church on Sunday afternoons to see that they were not thus used during service time. At Stogumber church, Somerset, an external bench-table runs the whole length of the north aisle ; in this instance the chief entrance to the church is on this side, and it has been suggested that this outside seat was provided for those who were listeners to a sermon from the churchyard cross in summer time.

It seems probable that the first permanent wooden church seats were those provided for the use of the priests and other clerks within the chancel during the quire offices ; they were provided with stone seats or sedilia on the south side of the altar, for use during High Mass, from Norman times downwards. There are a few of these chancel stalls extant which show Early English work of the thirteenth century. The custom, however, of supplying permanent wooden seats for any part of the congregation came about very gradually, and it possibly originated with the fixing of seats in chantry parcloses or guild chapels, and thus the custom spread to the general body of the church. We know that the habit obtained in certain churches before the close of the thirteenth century, especially in the West of England, of supplying a certain amount of general seating for the congregation, both from a few surviving examples, and also from record evidence.

In 1287 a synod was held at Exeter, under Bishop Quivil,

Atherington, Devon

F. S.

whereat an important ordinance was made as to seating, to the following effect, in a translated form :—

" Alas we have heard that, on account of seats in churches, the parishioners are often vexed, two or more persons claiming one seat. By reason of that grave scandal is generated in church and the divine office often impeded. We enact that no one from henceforth may claim a seat in church as his own ; noble persons and patrons of churches only excepted. He who for the cause of prayer shall first enter a church, let him select a place of prayer according to his will."

Just a few seats have come down to us of an early date. The benches at Dunsfold, Surrey, date from *c.* 1290 (171) ; four late thirteenth century dates have been assigned to those at Gaddesby, Leicestershire, and Clapton-in-Gordano, Somerset (147). At Aysgarth, West Riding, two beautifully pierced bench-ends of excellent Early English workmanship, ornamented with dog-tooth mouldings, were illustrated in the " Builder " on 27th July 1847. These bench-ends could not be of later date than *c.* 1250. In a later section of this book, dealing with old seating county by county, about half a dozen other instances of the survival of woodwork, possibly of the thirteenth century, are named.

In early Churchwardens' Accounts of the fifteenth century there are various references to pews which were obviously not for individuals of dignity, and which were old enough to need repair. Thus in 1447 there is an entry in the accounts of St Peter Cheap as to the " mendyng of a pew next the chirche door."

Fixed seats seem to have been called indifferently " pews," or " stalls," or "*seges.*" [1] In 1453, William Wintringham willed his body to be buried within a City church, *ad sedile vocati Angliæ* "*pewe,*" that is to say, beneath or by his wife's pew. In 1454-5 the several wives' seats in the accounts of St Ewen's, Bristol, are termed " sege," *e.g.,* " Robert Core for his Wyfe's Sege, vjd." John Young left ten marks in 1458 to Herne church, Kent, " to make seats called puyinge." At Ludlow, in 1542, 8s. 4d. was spent over the repairing and remaking of "the comyn pewis." The " Rites of Durham " speak of " the seat or pew where the Prior was accustomed to sit during Jesus Mass."

It may be as well here to interpose a few words as to the use and meaning of the term pew or pewing. The English word " pew " has for many a long year been associated with a seat or seats within a church ; yet Milton used the word to

---

[1] French *siège.*

W. P.　New Shoreham, Sussex

E. L. G.　Sutton Bonnington, Notts.

describe the sheep-pens of Smithfield, whilst Pepys applied it to a box at the theatre.   The word is somewhat indeterminate in its derivation, but Wedgewood, in his "Etymological Dictionary," is probably right in ascribing its origin to the Latin *podium*, a raised place.   See, however, the various long explanations and citations as to "Pew" in the "New English Dictionary."[1]   Taking the meaning to be an elevated or raised place, it is easy to see how it came to be used, not only for an official or dignified seat in a church, but also for a set of seats or benches affixed to a frame to raise them, though slightly, above the dampness of the actual floor level.

The word was in use long before the Reformation.   In the "Vision of Piers Plowman," *c.* 1360, Wrathe is made to state that he was accustomed to sit with wives and widows in church pews (*puwes*); but we need not fancy him shut up in a high pew with doors, but rather on an open bench.   Pew at that time was used less for a separate or official seat than for the whole system or block of seating.

Sir William Bruges, in 1449, made a bequest to the church of Stamford for "puying of the said church, not curiously but plainly."   In the same year the parish accounts of Thame contain the following specific entries :—

"For makyng of the setys yn ye northye quarter of
the chyrch at seynt jemys tyde   -   - xiijs. iiijd.
For makyng of the setys at Seynt hew ys tide   -   xiijs. iiijd.
Item to William karpentyre at Hocketyde -   - xiijs. iiijd.
For bed and borde or x days tym and ys childe   -   xvijd.
Item in bred and hale to men to helpe hym to drive
the setys to the wall   -   -   -   ijd.
Item to one of ys neyborys for the karyg of the
tymbyr from schyfton hedges man   -   - xvijd."

[1] The late Sir James Murray used occasionally to correspond with the writer as to the use of ecclesiastical terms.   In June 1905, when staying at Blythburgh, Suffolk, I received a letter from him, asking several questions as to the word "pew."   By a most strange coincidence, within an hour of the receipt of this letter I was visiting the village church of Reydon. Noticing an old horse-block built up after a curious fashion into the churchyard wall by the gateway, I asked a labourer passing by about it.   He replied, "Oh, I've heard that that there *horse-pew* was put there for farmers' wives to use when they rode on pillions."   This use of the word *pew* was confirmed by another passer-by.   I wrote that day to Sir James as to this incident.   The rule of this great dictionary is only to cite from printed matter, so the learned editor asked leave to send my statement to *Notes and Queries*.   It appeared there on 8th July 1905, and is duly quoted in the colossal work.

The bench-ends and seats were nearly always made from oak of first-rate quality, and are thick, strong, and heavy; oak was plentiful and cheap. Old oak does not rot, if protected from damp, and also properly ventilated; it simply crumbles away. The excellence of the old oak is largely due to its being cut in the winter, when there was little sap, and the bark was allowed

P. B. B.

Clapton-in-Gordano, Somerset

to remain.[1] Many of the benches, owing to their quality and massiveness, and the excellence of their construction, are in as good condition to-day as when first carved. Though the design of the benches varied greatly, especially in their ends, the actual construction and disposition usually remained the same, and consisted of a continuous sill laid along the floor, into which the

[1] *Reliquary*, x. 85.

2

bench-ends were stubbed, the seats being supported on brackets placed at intervals, with the backs either terminating level with the seats or carried down to the floor ; the book-board, often an addition of later days, was placed but little higher than the seat, and never slanting—in fact it was simply a ledge to lay the book on when not in use.[1]

At first the fixed seats seem to have formed quite small blocks, probably occupied only by women and infirm folk, and belonging to those who had defrayed the cost of putting them up.   Later, almost the whole of the nave and aisles, as far west-ward as the font, were frequently seated ; but to the end the aisles were usually left clear of seats.   Various instances are cited under a subsequent section where the old seats were complete, or nearly so, especially in East Anglia, and in the west counties of Somerset, Devon, and Cornwall.   Nearly all parochial naves possessed north and south doorways, one of which has frequently been blocked in modern times to stop the draughts.   The benches were arranged to leave a broad gangway down the nave from the one of these doorways to the other.   The longitudinal gangway of the nave was also considerably broader than in most modern churches.

Few realise what a wealth of old woodwork remains to us in spite of destructive "restorations."   There are believed to be a thousand carved bench-ends in Somerset alone ; there are probably as many in Devon ; and perhaps a larger number in Suffolk and Norfolk.   In East Anglia the primacy must be awarded to those of Wiggenhall St Mary the Virgin, Norfolk, and Fressingfield, Suffolk.   Those of Fressingfield are unequalled, alike in beauty of design and perfection of execution (163).

The ends, or standards, of the benches were often plain, with a moulded cornice, especially in the earlier examples.   But a vast number are elaborately panelled and carved.   A favourite subject in the later bench-ends, more particularly in Cornwall, are the symbols or instruments of the Passion, which lend them-selves to a great variety of design.   Thus the jug and ewer (as at Fressingfield) are significant of Pilate washing his hands at the *Condemnation.*   The *Betrayal* is typified by the sword, lantern, torch, club, thirty pieces of silver, and Malchus' ear. The actual *Passion* by the pillar of scourging, the scourges, the crown of thorns, the robe of mockery, the hammer, nails, sword, sponge, reed, spear, ladder, and pincers ; whilst St Peter's denial is brought to mind by the cock (15).

In East Anglia and elsewhere the bench-ends often rise into

---

[1] Brandon's "Analysis," p. 97.

C. H. E.

Holme, Notts.

C. H. E.

Balderton, Notts.

a finial termed the poppy-head ; but in the western counties the ends or standards are far more often horizontal (3).

The old bench-ends of our church seats, especially in the fifteenth century, frequently terminated in more or less ornamental or handsome finials, which have long been known as "Poppy-Heads" (5). Quite occasionally the rougher and smaller examples of these finials, as in some remote Lincolnshire churches, have a kind of resemblance to large poppy-heads of the opium type. As even the smell of the poppy is apt to induce slumber, there has been a good deal of would-be jocular writing in connection with these finials and sleeping in church during sermon time.[1] But this popular notion of the origin of the term is hopelessly wrong.

C. F. N.

Stowlangtoft, Suffolk

The name of poppy as here used is in reality an old French word, probably derived from the Latin *puppis*, which was the figure-head of a vessel, generally of an ornamental character; the word survives in our nautical term "poop." The figure-head suggested the idea of giving any carved head or finial a like title, whilst the French usually applied the word *poupée* to a child's doll, and afterwards especially to the wire-moved dancing dolls still called *poupettes*, or puppets in our language. To apply the term to the finial of a church seat is no mere modern conceit. In fact it is as old as the thirteenth century. An architect or designer of that century, one Wilars de Honcourt, has left behind him a curious MS., wherein he jotted down designs that took his fancy, including some bench finials, which he styles *poupées*. Hence writers on English Gothic adopted the slightly confusing term of "poppy-head." The

---

[1] "Penny Post," 11th February 1883.

C. F. N.　　　Great Walsingham, Norfolk

C. F. N.　　　Great Walsingham, Norfolk

" New Oxford Dictionary " throws doubt on this derivation, but
suggests nothing better, and is singularly barren in its quotations.
It cites two extracts from the parish accounts of St Mary-at-Hill
(City), under 1429 and 1512, the latter referring to a payment
for making " iij Mennys pewys, for the popeys and other stuff,
xxs." But it neglects to quote the 1450 accounts of the contract
for founding the Beauchamp chapel of St Mary's, Warwick,
wherein mention is made of the " Poppies, seats, sils," etc., for the
desks. Then, too, there is the valuable account of the expenses
of the founding of Corpus Christi College, Oxford, 1516, printed
by Hearne long ago in the appendix to his " History of
Glastonbury," wherein mention is made of the desks in the chapel,
which were to be made like those of Magdalen College chapel,
except that they were to be minus " the popie-heades."

The latest reference to poppy-heads in early Churchwardens'
Accounts occurs in 1572, when the church of St Martin-in-the-
Fields was repewed throughout with poppy-head benches :—

" Peyde for the Carvinge of xxvii. poppies-heads for
    the left side of the church   -   -   -   xxxvjs.
Peyde fore the Carvinge of xxv. for the right of the
    church -   -   -   -   -   -   xijs. viijd."

Poppy-heads are named as a matter with which archæologists
were quite familiar in Parker's " Glossary " of 1850. A certain
number of poppy-heads, especially in the chancels, are of
heterogeneous design ; e.g., circular knobs of flowers, kneeling
angels, figures of priests or bishops, or a variety of grotesque
monsters. The commonest form of the poppy-head is that of
the fleur-de-lis ; on this an infinite number of variations are
played, but the central motif is the same. The great frequency
of the fleur-de-lis type suggests that it may have been purposely
selected as the conventualised form of the lily, so constantly
represented in the Annunciation of the Blessed Virgin.

The benches were fixed in different ways. Occasionally
they were simply placed on the pavement of stone or of rammed
earth, and sometimes on a wooden flooring ; but most often they
were pinned to wooden plates. Occasionally they seem to have
been without backs, of which instances remain at Cawston (125),
East Winch, and Wissett, Norfolk, and even so late as those of
the chapel of Croydon hospital, founded by Archbishop Whitgift
in 1599. More often they had a back rail with a boarded or
panelled back, and as times advanced, in rich parishes, or where
particular benefactors were forthcoming, the backs of the seats
were carved or pierced with beautiful flowing patterns, as at the

Kilkhampton, Cornwall

Kilkhampton, Cornwall

Wiggenhalls, Norfolk, and Fressingfield, Suffolk; but more usually only the back or front seat of each block was thus treated, as at Dennington, Suffolk (166), and in many Devonshire and Somersetshire examples. These benches were fixed fairly wide apart; perhaps, as has been suggested, to allow uniformity to the practice of prostration as enjoined by the rubrics of the Sarum use, wherein it was ordered that the worshipper should *osculare terram aut formulam*, that is to say, "either kiss the ground or the form."

With regard to the number of quire stalls in many a small non-collegiate church, as often in the country churches of Norfolk, where there could not have been a staff of more than one or two priests, it should be remembered that the patron of the church not unfrequently claimed the right to a seat in the chancel. In fact in the mediæval days, such a claim was thoroughly recognised in the diocese of Durham as early as 1215. Even such a devout man as Sir Thomas More, at a far later period, was accustomed to sit in the chancel in right of his holding the office of Lord Chancellor, and a similar claim was made by several high officials in late pre-Reformation days. Lord Bacon tells us that "when Sir Thomas More was Lord Chancellor, he did use at Mass to sit in the chancel, and his lady in the pew, and upon the holy days during his High Chancellorship, one of his gentlemen, when the service of the church was done, used to come to my Lady his wife's pew door, and say unto her, 'Madam, my Lord is gone.'" Lord Bacon proceeds to state that he abandoned this custom on the day he gave up the charge of the Great Seal.

This custom of granting a single seat in the chancel to the patron or the leading layman of the parish was monstrously exaggerated in post-Reformation days, when it was the common habit of the squires to insist upon having a great pew for themselves and their families within the chancel. It is stated that at Swanscombe church, Kent, up to its restoration in 1873, the whole of the south side of the long chancel was occupied by a splendidly upholstered pew, with table and chairs, wherein sat a dignified tenant farmer, as the representative of the lord of the important manor of Swanscombe; whilst the north side of the chancel was equally divided between the rector and the lord of the tributary manor of Alkerden in the same parish. But this subject is dealt with in detail in the subsequent account of manorial pews.

CHAPTER II

Separation of the Sexes—Flap Seats—Special Pews—Shriving Pew—Churching or Midwife's Pew—Maiden's Pew—Bride's Pew—Movable Pews—Pews Locked ; Stamped with Initials or Names—Seat Rents at St Lawrence, Reading ; at St Edmund's, Salisbury ; Ashton-under-Lyne ; Eccles—Protests against Irreverence and Luxury in Churches—John Mayre—Sir Thomas More—Bishop Bentham—Bishop Lockett—Sir Christopher Wren.

THE separation of the sexes during Christian worship goes back to the very dawn of Christianity. The author of the "Apostolic Constitution" says : "Let the doorkeepers stand at the gate of the men, and the deaconesses at the gate of the women." St Augustine clearly intimates that each sex had its distinct place assigned to it ; and an incident in the life of St Ambrose establishes the same thing. We read of the Empress Helena praying with the women in their part of the church. Complete separation of the sexes is still rigorously maintained throughout the various Churches of the East.

In England, as is well known, the sexes were strictly separated in our old churches ; the men were usually seated on the south side, and the women on the north. At Wiggenhall St Mary the Virgin, Norfolk, this is made quite plain by the carving of the figures in the niches of the elaborate bench-ends ; for in the southern block of benches in the nave only male saints are represented, whilst those on the north side contain a representation of the Blessed Virgin (126). The same arrangements were continued by the Reformers. In 1549 the first Prayer Book of Edward VI. ordered that "So many as shall be partakers of the Holy Communion shall tarry still in the quire, the men on one side, and the women on the other side."

In 1620 one Mr Loveday of St Alphege, Cripplegate Within, was brought to book because that he had sat in the same pew with his wife ; his conduct was held to be "highly indecent." The order is extant as to the allotment of seats in the little country church of Ashford, Derbyshire, under date 10th April

3

1632. The names of all the men and women in the parish appear to be entered. " Under the pulpitt is for the minister's wife whomsoever she is." On the north side, in the " place next the queer," were the wives of three yeomen. In the three pews behind them sat other women who are styled " Goodwife." The men were placed on the south side.

C. F. N.

Clovelly, Devon

In 1638, at his visitation, Bishop Montague of Norwich made inquiry, " Do men and women sit together, indifferently and promiscuously ? or, as the fashion was of old, do men sit together upon one side of the church and women upon the other ? " In the parish register of Stoke Hammond, Bucks., for 1672, is a whole page devoted to allotting the seats to the parishioners by name ; the men on the south side, the women on the north.

Instances might easily be multiplied in country parishes

up and down England where the separation of the sexes, in whole or in part, prevailed down to our own days, not only in churches, but even in certain of the smaller modern Non-conformist chapels. It is a matter of common knowledge that it is now the custom in a fair number of town churches.

A curiosity of early seating was the way in which flap seats, as they are usually termed, were attached to the ends of the substantial standards of the more permanent seating. Many instances of this kind of seating could be quoted from Wardens' Accounts of the seventeenth century. Thus, in 1627-8, at St Edmund's, Salisbury, there is an entry of "Goody Langley for a small hanging seate 6 pence." We are able to show an illustration of the flap seating at Tintinhull, Somerset, where the flaps are attached to the bench-ends (22) of the year 1511. Such seats were by no means intended for any chance comer, but were strictly assigned ; for the most part to the maids of the occupants of the permanent pew, or in some cases to the children. In the parish accounts of St Oswald, Durham, it was ordered in 1608—"That no man younge or olde shall in tyme of Divine Service sytt upon the sides and edges of womens stales upon payne of ijd." An entry with regard to the use of these subsidiary seats occurs in Archdeacon Hale's " Proceedings in the Diocese of London," where it is stated of a young woman named Hayward, "that she beinge a young mayde sat in the pewe with her mother, to the great offence of reverent women ; howbeit that after I, Peter Lewis, the Vicar, had in the church privatlie admonished the said young mayde of her fault, and advised her to sitt at her mothers pewe dore, she obeyed, but now she sitts againe with her mother." At a later date a few of these extra seats were made permanent by the insertion of a bracket beneath them ; an instance of this occurs in the church of Clovelly, North Devon. In 1651-2, in an elaborate new scheme for seating, in the oft-cited accounts of St Edmund's, Salisbury, there are various entries relative to such seats :—

" Mrs Ann Carter, hanging seat for servant 1s.—Josse, wife of Perigan Dawes, sliding seat before Magistrates' Pew 2s. 6d. — Mrs Battes, widow, a flap seat fixt to her owne for servant 6d."

Special pews for particular objects are occasionally mentioned in late post-Reformation accounts, such as a shriving pew. The following are references to a pew of this description in the City churches :—

"1493-4 (*St Mary-at-Hill*) for a matt for the shreivyng
    pewe -   -   -   -   -   -   -   iijd.
1499-1500 (*St Andrew Hubbard*) for gere for the shryv
    yng pewe   -   -   -   -   -   jd.
1511 (*St Margaret Pattens*) a clothe for Lent, to hang
    before the screvyng pewe   -   -   -   -
1515 Dressynge the yrons of the shrevyng pew   -   jd.
1548 (*St Michael, Cornhill*) to the joyner for takynge
    down the shryvyng pew, and making another pew
    in the same place   -   -   -   -   -   iijs."

It has usually been assumed that this shriving pew was some
form of a confessional; but it can be shown from various
illustrations and other records that it was the custom in the
mediæval Church of England to hear confession at the chancel
screen or within the chancel. We think it far more likely that
this shriving pew was the appointed place for those to sit who
were awaiting their turn to be shrived. It is at the present
day the custom in divers churches, where the habit of auricular
confession prevails, to have seats assigned for those waiting to
make their confession, both men and women, more particularly
at Shrovetide or before Easter.

A sixteenth century custom, continued long after that period,
was to have a pew termed the churching pew, or sometimes the
midwife's pew, because it was usual for the midwife to accom-
pany the woman to church on that occasion. There was, of
course, no necessity for such a pew under the Commonwealth,
when churching was abolished.

"1538-9 (*St Mary, Dover*) Paid for the pullynge downe of
    the chyldewyffes pew of Saynt Martyns Church,
    and for the bryngyng of hit home -   -   -   iijd.
1617 (*St Margaret, Westminster*) Midwives Pew   - £2. 5s.
1634 (*Campsall, Yorks*) A Childwife Pew   -   - 26s. 8d.
1646-7 (*St Thomas, Sarum*) For the Midwives old Pew
    for Ric. Bristow   -   -   -   -   -   20s.
1683 (*Edenbridge*) Pd. to Thomas Wells for a matt and
    a Trott for the Churching Seate   -   -   - 6s. 8d."

The custom was, before the Reformation, to take the service
at the church door. The "quire door" was substituted in 1549.
"The place where the table standeth" was the order in 1552.
In 1662 it was altered to "some convenient place as hath
been accustomed, or as the Ordinary shall direct." The churching pew often stood in the chancel near to the altar; this was
the case at Luccombe, Somerset, up to its restoration in 1843.

A further distinction was made not only between the sexes, but between married and unmarried women. The young women and girls usually sat by themselves; there are various sixteenth century accounts of City churches bearing this out. At St Mary Woolchurch, in 1541-2, occurs this item : " Paid for mending the maydens pewe in the church, ijs."

A special pew, occasionally mentioned in early parish accounts, was devoted to those who were seeking matrimony. Thus at Chester-le-Street is the following entry under 27th May 1612 : " The churchwardens meeting for seeking for workmen to mak a seete in a convenient place for brydgrumes, brydes and sike wyves to sit in, two shillings." A document at Warrington church, Lancashire, dated 1628, as to an allotment of seats, refers to " the brydes form."

In some few cases movable pews were placed in our churches in the late seventeenth or early eighteenth century days, and must have been convenient for cleaning purposes. Previous to the restoration, *c.* 1860, the small church of Chelmorton, Derbyshire, was fitted with pews which were movable, and each entirely distinct from its neighbour. They were constructed of oak with sides, ends, and a floor an inch or two above the ground level. One of the ends formed a door. They could be moved or lifted about at pleasure. Mr Llewellyn Jewitt, in describing them, wrote that " they were placed side by side in the church, and looked more like a number of old-fashioned children's beds or cribs than anything else." In most instances the name or initials of the owners were carved on the door. The drawing is from a sketch made by Mr Jewitt, which appeared in the 1876 volume of the Anastatic Drawing Society, Pl. XLII. The door of the pew bears the name T. Buxton, with the conjoined initials of " TEB," and " TE, TB," and the date 1703.

In Cartmell there used to be a pew, the Wraysholme Tower pew, which rolled on four large oak ball castors ; it was obviously intended to be moved when desired.[1]

The selfish and unchristian idea of excluding fellow-worshippers from a particular pew seems to have suggested the cheap expedient of putting an iron bar across the ends of two benches, thereby proving that exclusiveness, when worshipping one common Father, is not a mere product of quasi-modern times. At Bishop's Hull, Somerset, may be seen several old benches with an iron bar fitting across the ends. From the bar the transition is short to a more effective barrier, the door, which

---

[1] Rigge's " Cartmell," p. 7.

C. F. N.   Tintinhull, Somerset

C. F. N.   Tintinhull, Somerset

wealth of the occ
being duly enter
were allotted to
sixty-three wom
women in the ba
men were allotte
8d. each in the n
each, five wome
women in the ne
each in the three
women were allo

A considerab
of St Edmund, S
in pews. We k
scandal of map
accordance with
attained to such
shown to have o
innocent beginni
and it is not un
three seats. In
was for the mo
year onwards th
word " Pewes " f
had sprung up to
good wiefe of th
following year "
had to pay 2s. fo
entry as to the
1629 it was resol

" All the po
Church Poore s
orders made upo
Churchwardens a
that weekes pa
Formes may be
these wordes pai
the Poore."

In connectio
mention that the
tion of seats, i
holders, occurre
Lancashire man

At Eccles, I
churchwardens s

4

at first was low. When Tattershall church, Lincolnshire, was rebuilt in 1455, the benches were provided with low doors. Yet there must have been doors in some churches earlier than this; for in 1466, at St Michael's, Cornhill, they had been in the church so long that they were much out of repair, and the church-wardens *"payed to a carpenter for mending of the pewes and dores v^s v^d."*

Then came the natural English wish to lock the door; and the wish was gratified the very next year, when the same churchwardens *"payd to a smith for mayking of a lok to Maister Stokkens pew . . . viij^d."*

With regard to this locking of pews, it may be remarked that in 1600 the churchwardens' pew at St John Zachary, London, was supplied with two keys; four years later several keys were provided for the burgesses' pews at St Margaret's, Westminster. Bishop Earle of Exeter, in 1628, alluded to this evil practice in his description of the character of " *The She Precise Hypocrite,"* stating that "she doubts of the Virgin Mary's salvation, and dares not saint her; but knows her own place in heaven as perfectly as the pew she has a key to."

In 1631, on 21st May, Bishop Neile of Winchester issued a monition on this subject to the wardens of Elvetham, Hants: " Whereas I am given to understand that locks have lately been sett upon some pews in the parish church of Elvetham, and that without any order from me or my chancellor, which I hould very unfitt to be indured, these are to will and require you and every of you the churchwardens there, to remove all lockes upon any of the pews within the said church between this and the feast day of Pentecost next insuing."

At a somewhat later period, Pepys speaks of a practice of locking pews as a common custom: " December 25, 1661. In the morning to church where at the door of our pew I was fain to stay, because the sexton had not opened the door."

The co-religionists being locked out, the next thing was to stamp the pew as private property, the owner's initials being branded on it, as on sheep and pig. There is a record for 1550 in a London church: " *Paide for wrytinge on the pewe dores at my Lorde of London's commandement, xijd."* Seats with initials on them occur at Hurstpierpoint, Sussex, Stogumber, Somerset, and in nearly a hundred other cases. At North Thoresby, Lincolnshire, early in the seventeenth century, there were put up benches whose ends bear the initials of the farmers to whom they were appropriated; one has a medallion, probably of the occupier.

In this way pews or benches became private property, and

were boug
few such
Yeovil, S
the pulpi
whole of
formally
to sit in
shuld be
deyned fo
the charg
The
England
House o
by wealt
cent mot
of St L
others, te
of wome
with an a
ment wa
Rolls of
year 14
setell " 1
by three
for the e
6s. 6d., v
ing to w
women
range, a
pay bu'
day as
mayors
The
" Ite
By '
of Reac
a man (
the ma
gatewa
mother
The
movem
tinued
the par
House

and also for the vicar, according to their degrees and calling, and in like manner shall have authority to place the rest of the parishioners, as well husbandmen and cottagers, as others of mean estate and calling ; having a special regard for their charges and payments which they have severally paid towards the repair of the said church and making anew of the said forms."

John Mayre, when writing his " Instructions for Parish Priests" (Early English Text Society, 1868), in the fifteenth century, had

E. K. P.

Poltimore, Devon

occasion to comment on the irreverent behaviour of those men of the congregation who lolled about lounging against the pillars. He says that men should put away all vanity :—

> " Ne mon in chyrche stonde schal,
> Ny lene to pyler, ne to wal,
> But fayre on knees they schall hem sette
> Knelynge down up on the flette.
>
> .   .   .   .   .   .
>
> And whenne the Gospelle red he schalle
> Teche hem thenne to stande up alle."

Many a protest was entered by the more devout folk against the increasing comfort and luxury that was aimed at in the later pre-Reformation days during the services of the Church. The good Sir Thomas More protested against the ease that was sought for even by those kneeling : " If it hap us to kneel, then either do kneel upon the one knee and lean upon the tother, or else we have a cushion laid under them both ; yea, sometimes, if we be anything nice and fine, we call for a cushion to bear up our elbows ; like an old, rotten, ruinous house, be ye fain to be staid and underpropped." Bishop Bentham of Lichfield (1560-79), in his visitations, directed the people " not to walk up and down in the church, not to jangle, babble, nor talk in church time, but to give diligent attention to the priest."

The fashion of the pews of the next century called forth an indignant reproof from Bishop Corbett of Norwich (1633-6): "Stately pews are now become tabernacles with rings and curtains to them. There wants nothing but beds to hear the Word of God on; we have casements, locks and keys and cushions—I had almost said bolsters and pillows ; and for these we love the church." One more protest against pews shall be cited. Sir Christopher Wren, in 1708, boldly writes : —

"A church should not be so filled with pues, but that the poor may have some room in the alleys to stand and sit in ; for to them equally is the Gospel preached. It is to be wished that there were no pews, but benches. But there is no stemming the tide of profit, and the advantage of the pew-keepers ; especially too since by Pews, in the Chapels of Ease, the Minister is chiefly supported."

CHAPTER III

THE present writer drew attention, more than a score of years ago, to the fact that the big manorial or squire's pews, from Elizabethan times downwards, had for the most part their origin in the Church usages of mediæval days. From an early period it was the custom of various landed proprietors, or of those who had become wealthy through trade, to found chantries in connection with their parish church, wherein priests, specially endowed, said masses for their good estate when living, but more especially for their souls after death, and for the souls of their ancestors. Such chantry chapels not infrequently took the form of adjuncts to either side of the chancel, or formed transepts, but as time went on they were more often formed by parclose screens at the east end of the aisles, of which a few remain. Striking instances of chantry enclosures still used and known as "pews" occur in the fine church of Lavenham, Suffolk, where there are the De Vere and the Spring pews, the founder of the former being the Earl of Oxford, the lord of the manor, and the latter a wealthy local clothier (29). Within the old chantry parclose or screen there used to stand an altar with room not only for the celebrant and his clerk, but also for seats with desks for the founder and his dame, and afterwards for their descendants. When chantries were abolished in 1519, the chantry space was retained by the lord of the manor or the family of the founder, and ere long developed into the square pew or enclosure wherein the family could sit in state and privacy for the ordinary services of the Reformed Church. By degrees it came about that the smaller squirearchy, the professional man, the yeoman farmer, the successful teacher, and above all, the wife and family of the married priest, desired to imitate the great man of the parish; and hence somewhat small boxes or squared pews grew up in the rear of the big manorial pew.

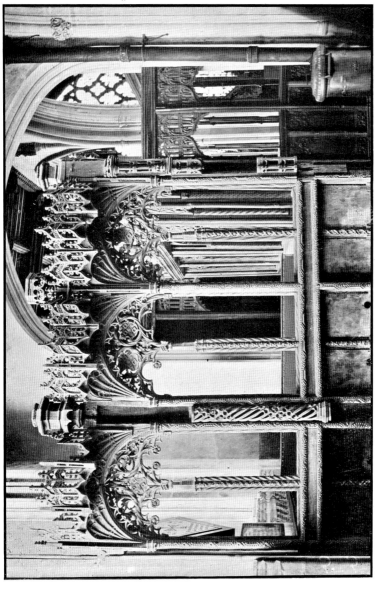

Lavenham, Suffolk

G. G. B.

At *Wensley*, Yorkshire, the remarkable Scrope pew is mainly composed of screen work which formerly surrounded the Scrope chantry in Easby abbey. The elaborate screen and enclosed pews at the east end of the nave of *Whalley* church, Lancashire, are undoubtedly survivors of late chantries. In the small church of *Cartmell Fell*, in the same county, there are two enclosed areas or pews ; the one on the north side has a dilapidated screen of pre-Reformation date, and was probably a chantry parclose (33). At the north-east end of *Kedington* church, Suffolk, stands the manorial canopied pew of the Bernadiston family ; three sides of this large square pew are of early seventeenth century work, but the side facing south is Gothic, showing tracery, *c.* 1500. This latter part is usually supposed to have come from a destroyed rood-screen, but in our opinion it is part of the pre-Reformation chantry parclose which stood on this site. At the east end of the north aisle of *Haltham* church, Lincolnshire, there is some fine late fifteenth century carving enclosing a space for a chantry, which has always been used as a pew ; the curious thing about it is that a comparatively narrow pew or enclosure is continued some little way along the outer wall at right angles to the main part : the carving of this latter part seems to be coeval with the rest. There is a remarkable canopied and enriched pew at *Madley*, Herefordshire, apparently Elizabethan, but there is early tracery, probably pertaining to an older chantry enclosure. In several cases, as at *Ightham*, Kent, there are some rows of seats within parclose screens which still occupy their original position.

To make the state pew still more cosy and proudly distinctive from the rest of the church, the fashion set in during the latter part of the sixteenth century, and throughout most of the following century, of roofing it in with a canopy. The canopied Elizabethan pew in the midst of the north aisle of the fascinating Leicestershire church of *Breedon* is a good example ; it is the property of Earl Ferrers. Of Elizabethan date, but eminently non-English, is the striking and beautiful pew enclosure in the Devonshire church of *Holcombe Rogus* ; it is quite *sui generis*, and is cinquecento work of Italian style, though possibly made in England. The summit is adorned with medallions of scriptural subjects with clear backgrounds ; perhaps the best and simplest of the subjects is the " Return of the Two Spies " ; the whole merits close study (37, 39). Eminently associated with Elizabeth is the historic, but, alas ! disused chapel of *Rycote*, in the Oxfordshire parish of Haseley. This chapel, founded in 1449, was used by the Princess Elizabeth when she was a prisoner here under Queen Mary, and also by Charles I.

Brancepeth, Durham

C. E. S.

during his prolonged stay at Oxford. The position of the rood-screen is now occupied by two elaborately carved Renaissance pews. The pew on the south side with a coved canopy or tester was probably erected for the princess, and the one on the north for the ill-fated king. The latter is of two storeys, the upper is gained by the old rood-loft stairs. The upper part, which is a good deal mutilated, probably served for the organ (38).

So soon as the occupation of former chantry chapels had been legitimised, lords of the manor and other magnates began

L. B.

Chorley, Lancs.

to transform them, or to erect pews where there had been no chantry, often raising the height, or adopting other measures, such as curtains, to secure their privacy from the gaze of ordinary Christians. The raising of canopies over these great pews caused them to assume the appearance of four-post bedsteads, a likeness which induced Swift thus to satirise them in " Baucis and Philemon ":—

> "A bedstead of the antique mode,
> Compact of timber many a load,
> Such as our ancestors did use,
> Was metamorphosed into pews ;
> Which still their ancient nature keep
> By lodging folk disposed to sleep."

Cartmell Fell, Lancashire

There is a near approach to the four-poster in the remarkable manorial pew of *Tawstock*, Devon, of which we give a front view (41).

It is difficult to discriminate between later Elizabethan and early Jacobean work. In this category we are inclined to put the fine uncanopied pew of *South Hayling*, Hants, with linenfold panels in the lower tier; the elaborate great pews of *Laxfield*, Suffolk, and *Chelvey*, Somerset, together with the series of pews on the south side of *Mudford*, in the latter county.

The manorial pew of *Crowcombe*, Somerset, in connection with the stately screen and pulpit, which we know to be of the year 1616, is a fine example of pure Jacobean carving. Almost equally good is the carving of approximate date on the two state pews just through the screen of *Ashby St Ledgers*, Northants. There are two good dated examples of Carolean carving of manor pews, the one, 1627, at *Burneston*, North Riding, Yorks., and the other, 1635, at *Herriard*, Hants, where it now serves as an organ screen. Later instances in the seventeenth century are the good canopied pew at *Stokesay*, Salop (46); the pew parclose on the north side of the nave of *Ellingham*, Hants; the Parker pew and Standiall pew at *Chorley*, Lancashire, the latter with a canopy supported on spirally twisted shafts, which shows it to be post-Restoration (32); the curious canopied pew on the south side of the chancel of *Cartmell Fell*, with a latticed cornice supported on tall turned shafts; and the still later manorial pew, *c.* 1700, at *High Ongar*, Essex.

L. B.

Chorley, Lancs.

J. D.

Croft, Yorkshire

It remains to add another paragraph concerning one or two of the more exceptional or peculiar manorial pews. The story and condition of the old Bampfylde pew at *Poltimore*, Devon, are not a little remarkable. This old family, still resident at Poltimore Park close to the church, and now represented by Lord Poltimore, coolly appropriated to themselves, immediately after the Reformation, the old rood-loft on the top of the chancel screen. The church is cruciform, with a south aisle added, and the old Bampfylde chantry occupied the south arm, where their monuments and burial crypt still remain. After a while the rood-loft seat was abandoned, and a big pew was built up partly over the site of the chantry, 7 ft. from the floor of the church, and originally gained by the old rood-loft stair-way. When the south aisle was built in modern days, and the old screen unfortunately moved during a poor restoration, a new oak staircase had to be constructed to gain the great pew, starting from the end of the new aisle. This extraordinary and unseemly pew has a moulded ceiling 7 ft. 6 in. above the pew floor, and is panelled in oak at the front, back, and sides, and it is provided with a fire-place (of comparatively modern date) and everything tending to comfort. The whole area measures 10 ft. by 9 ft., and it is lined throughout with red cloth. The north arm of the transept was formerly provided with a somewhat similar gallery pew, for the use of the retainers of the Bampfylde family, exactly opposite, but this has lately been removed (26).

At *Newton St Cyres*, near Exeter, there is another of these "furnished apartments" pews, the furniture quite new, the squire having recently (1908) substituted ten upholstered chairs and a centre-table in the place of the old benches. At *Kenton*, in the same county, the squire's pew is wonderfully upholstered; but perhaps the worst case of a furnished modern manorial pew, with separate entrance, occurs under the west tower of *Enville*, Staffordshire. The manorial pew of *Selworthy*, Somerset, is the chamber over the south porch, gained by the old stairway in the wall; the wall into the church was removed in the middle of the eighteenth century, and an alcove thrown out into the church. The present writer has often seen the celebrated old Sir Thomas Acland, so popular in the west (grandfather of the present Sir Thomas), standing out in the forefront of this pew, almost leading the singing of the adjacent village orchestra, in the west gallery of the same date as the pew, with his stentorian voice (47). The church of *Croft*, North Riding, Yorks., is much disfigured by an extraordinary and essentially vulgar elevated manorial pew erected on pillars by the Milbanks about the middle of the eighteenth century (35). It is reached by a wide and

Holcombe Rogus, Devon

F. H. C.

preposterous balustraded staircase, which stretches out into the
open church; on the occasion of our visit it was carpeted in
bright red, secured by glossy brass stair-rods. Altogether it
struck us as the most ghastly, and almost profane pew in the
kingdom, especially as comfortless-looking seats at the far
back of the church were ostentatiously labelled "For the Poor."
What a comment on St James ii. 2, 3! These great manorial

W. M.

Rycote, Oxon.

pews are dying out, but at least a score possessing fire-places,
tables, armchairs, and in one case a sofa, and for the most part
having a separate entrance, still linger.

Bloxworth, Dorset, has a large manorial pew with a fire-place,
apparently glorying in its exclusiveness. It is adorned with
the arms of the Savage family, from Rock Savage, Chester, who
were lords of the manor from the middle of the sixteenth
century down to 1700.

Holcombe Rogus, Devon

F. H. C.

It must, however, in all fairness be remembered that such things are not altogether products of post-Reformation times. In the north of the chancel of Stoke d'Abernon, Surrey, a chantry chapel was erected in the days of Henry VII., and it possesses the strange adjunct of a Tudor fire-place; but we believe this to be unique in pre-Reformation days. Yet there was evidently a desire for an excess of comfort and of distinction in church among certain of our forefathers. There is evidence that great people yearned, or were supposed to yearn, for ease within the church walls as early as the first half of the fifteenth century. In the " Booke of Nurture," written in 1420 by John Russell, steward to the Duke of Gloucester, the following advice is given to a chamberlain as to preparing for his master attending church :—

> " Pryore or prelate if hit be, or any other potentate,
> Or he enter in to the churche, be it erly or late,
> Perceive all thynges for his pewe that yt be made preparate,
> Both cosshyn, carpet, and curteyne, bedes and boke, forget not these."

The grand pews and their costly fittings, which came into vogue in post-Reformation times, were as a rule paid for by their respective proprietors; but this was not always the case, especially in towns, as may be gathered from the two following excerpts from Elizabethan Churchwardens' Accounts :—

St Martin's, Leicester, 1563-4—

> " Pd. to Thomas Oliver for a daye worke aboute my
>   lordes seate (Earl of Huntingdon)   -   -   xd.
> Pd. to them wch holpe us about mi lordes seate   -   jd.
> Pd. for mattes for my lordes chappel -   -   iiijs. iiijd.
> Pd. for a skin of red lether and halfe a thosand red
>   neles for mi lordes seate   -   -   -   -   xvjd.
> Pd. to Michael Parker for v yerds of broade grene,
>   and iij quarters of narrow grene for my lordes
>   seate   -   -   -   -   -   -   vjs. ijd."

St Stephen Walbrook, 1577—

> " For Alderman Bondes pewe, viz. xxxi yeardes greene saie
> at xvjd. beyeard, xlis. iiijd. : for xvi dozen of lace at viijd. the
> doz. xs. viijd. : Three workmen ij daies apiece, xijd. : ij mattes
> xxd. : Candels j pound, iijd. : for Coles, viijd. : Bredd beare and
> butter, xijd. : To a painter, vjd. : Nales vli., vs. : Paid to a
> Carpenter, iijd.   In all the charges of this pew, iijli. xiijs. vd."

F. S.

Tawstock, Devon

6

Examples may also be cited from town parish accounts as to the expenditure in providing seats or pews of dignity for corporation officials. A single one must suffice as to the Lord Mayor and Lady Mayoress of the City in Elizabethan days :—

St Peter Cheap, 1572—

" For payntinge over my ladye mayres pewe   -   -   xs.

For a piece of sages for my lorde mayres and my ladyes pewes   -   -   -   -   -   xls.

For lattyn nayles and black nayles for my lorde mayres pewe and my ladyes   -   -   -   iijd.

For lace for them Twos pews -   -   -   -   iijs.

To a plasterer for whiting over my ladye mayres pewe   xxd.

To the joyner for the silke for my lord mayres pewe   -   -   -   -   -   iijli. xs. iijd.

For xijli. of flax to make ij settills for my lorde mayres and my layde mayres pewe at iijd. ob.   -   iiid."

A chapter on Esquires' pews would scarcely be complete without mentioning a curious circumstance connected with the repewing of *Kirkby Malham*, Yorks., early in the eighteenth century. At the west end of the nave are two large pews, one for the churchwardens, and the other, on the north side, for the esquires. On the latter is inscribed " Esq^{rs} 1724, T. L. (Thomas Lister), W. S. (William Serjeantson), L. C., C. W. (Charles Waddington)."

CHAPTER IV

GALLERIES

IN considering the seating of a church, galleries must not be omitted. Even before the Reformation a few galleries had already been erected beneath western towers, *e.g.*, at Worstead (1501), Aylsham, and Cawston, Norfolk. At Cromer, South Repps, and a few other Norfolk churches, though the galleries have gone, there are doorways to the newel staircase of the western tower low down, which can only have opened into galleries. Mildenhall, Suffolk, has a fine fan-vaulted gallery of stone under the western tower. The west gallery of Branscombe church, Devon, is a fine piece of work, *c.* 1600 ; we are glad to say that it was spared during a recent restoration. To these western galleries beneath the towers many a choir doubtless was transferred which previously had sat in the chancel or the rood-loft. The next step, to get more room, was to erect the gallery, not beneath the tower, but in front of the tower arch, right across the nave. From this it was an easy transition to continue it right and left, as at Old Woking and Collumpton, right across the aisles as well. Such a gallery would accommodate a considerable part of the congregation as well as the choir. In rapidly growing places the mere increase of population led to supplementing the accommodation of the church by galleries. Thoresby, in his " Diary," says that in the early part of the seventeenth century the churches in Leeds were so full " that they were constrained to build new seats and lofts," *i.e.*, " galleries." Even where the population had not grown so much, the introduction of the great square pews so seriously curtailed the congregational area that galleries seemed unavoidable.

Churchstanton, Somerset

G. I. G.

Puddletown, Dorset

C. F. N.

When once, however, a gallery had been erected at the west, there soon followed side galleries to the north and south of the nave. There were even put up here and there galleries at the east end of the nave; *i.e.*, under or in front of the chancel arch, as in St Mary Magdalene, Taunton. When this was done, the nave was galleried all round, very much like a theatre. And when, in addition, a flat whitewashed ceiling was put up under the open timber roof as a protection from draughts, the eighteenth

T. C.

Stokesay, Salop

century Christians had a church which suited them precisely: cosy, comfortable, and stuffy, with every trace of Catholic mediævalism put out of sight. It is hardly possible now to realise the shocking state of our galleried churches up to the Gothic revival of the last century. Not only small village churches, but great town churches, collegiate churches, such as Beverley minster, and even the quires of cathedrals were blocked up with monstrous galleries. Here and there an example survives still; *e.g.*, at Whitby and Monkwearmouth.

O. C.

Selworthy, Somerset

The erection of galleries did not go on without occasional active opposition. In 1606 the Mayor and Council put up a gallery for themselves in Bristol cathedral, near the pulpit. Bishop Thornborough pulled it down because "it made the church look like a playhouse." In 1608 he was compelled to reconstruct it ; but he put it only 3 ft. from the pavement, and removed the pulpit so far away that the Mayor and Corporation could not hear the sermon. In 1635, Wren, then Bishop of Hereford, asks, "Are there galleries? Is not the church large enough without them to receive all your own parishioners? Is any part of the church hidden or darkened thereby, or any in your parish annoyed or offended by them?" Some of the bishops insisted on having the galleries taken down. In 1641 a Puritan committee of the House of Lords strongly complained of the "taking down galleries in churches, and restraining the building of such galleries where the parishes are very populous." However, the opinions of church folk changed after the Restoration, and a large number of western galleries were put up, of oak, and sometimes marked by considerable beauty of detail. Later, in the eighteenth century, came in deal and graining, together with cheapness and nastiness.

The following are seventeenth century dated examples of western galleries, several of the first of which are distinctly good of their kind :—

Wolverhampton (1610); Lyme Regis (1611); Woking, Surrey (1622); Newdegate, Surrey (1627); Watlington, Berks. (1630); Odiham, Hants (1632); Leighton Buzzard (1634); Moreton Say, Shropshire (1634); Middletown, Dorset (1635); Gressenhall, Norfolk (1635); East Brent, Somerset (1635); Bishop's Cleeve, Gloucester (1640); Upton Magna, Shropshire (1666). There are also good eighteenth century galleries at Selworthy, Somerset, and at Shere, Surrey. The fine west gallery of Branscombe, Devon, is *c.* 1500.

PART II

CHAPTER V

Bench - Ends and Stalls: Bedfordshire, Berkshire, Buckinghamshire, Cambridgeshire, Cheshire, Cornwall, Cumberland, Derbyshire, Devon, Dorset, Durham, Essex, Gloucestershire, Hampshire, Herefordshire, Hertfordshire, Huntingdonshire, Lancashire, Leicestershire, Lincolnshire, Middlesex, Norfolk, Northamptonshire, Northumberland, Nottinghamshire, Oxfordshire, Rutland, Shropshire, Somerset, Suffolk, Surrey, Sussex, Warwick, Wiltshire, Worcester, Yorkshire, Wales.[1]

BEDFORDSHIRE

THE small county of BEDFORDSHIRE is not remarkable for either the number or character of its bench-ends; but there are one or two churches with fairly noteworthy examples. First among them may be mentioned *Stevington*, pleasantly situated on the west bank of the Ouse, some two miles to the west of Oakley station. Attention was drawn to the quaintness of the Stevington bench-ends so long ago as 1812, when such matters aroused but little curiosity. A correspondent of the "Gentleman's Magazine" furnished a drawing of the heads of two of them to the eighty-second volume, and gives an unnecessarily coarse description

---

[1] The following lists of examples of carved bench-ends and of various forms of old wooden seating are arranged alphabetically under the different counties of England, and collectively for those of Wales. It should, however, be clearly understood that no claim is made for completeness, especially in such counties as Norfolk, Suffolk, Devon, and Somerset, where they abound ; but as the writer has given so much of a long lifetime to the examination of our old churches, having visited the whole of the ancient parish churches in at least eleven counties, it is hoped and believed that the omissions of important instances are at least few and far between.

of the figures, which are certainly of an unusual character, and
more suited for the generally veiled grotesques of the under sides
of misericords than for the broad daylight of the tops of the ends
of nave benches.   On the summits of these bench-ends are
small figures of men drinking, sleeping, and reading in quaint
attitudes, whilst others are carved with quadrupeds.   We give
two examples on page 51.   They are of fifteenth century date.

In the interesting church of *Houghton Conquest* a good deal
of fifteenth century traceried panelling is preserved in the
pewing, reconstructed during a very drastic restoration by Sir
Gilbert Scott in 1870.   The chancel stalls have ends with poppy-
head finials of unusual design.   It is fair to notice these in a
book on bench-ends rather than in the volume of the series on
chancel stalls, for we have been assured by a resident, who well
remembered the restoration, that these bench ends with poppy-
heads were all removed from the nave.

The fine Perpendicular church of *Eaton Socon* has a remarkable series of bench-ends with bold early fifteenth century
poppy-heads, mostly of original design.   They represent a
number of different beasts, but the best are cunningly carved with
foliage and small human figures (53).

In *Yeldon* church the traceried heads of the pulpit panels
are *c.* 1500, and some of the pew ends are of like design and
date.   At *Keysoe* there are a number of early sixteenth century
bench-ends in the nave, and in the north aisle of *Clapham* church
are three old bench-ends, whilst at *Cople* there is some late
sixteenth century pewing both in the nave and in the north
aisle.

A few more Bedfordshire churches may be quite briefly
named in alphabetical order, for each of these contain certain
seating of interest to the student of ecclesiastical woodwork.
Bolnhurst, some fifteenth century nave pewing ; *Bromham*, some
old bench-ends in the nave, varnished over, and in the chancel
two old standards with double-faced finials ; *Carlton*, much of
the nave pewing sixteenth century ; *Chellington*, some seventeenth
century benches in the aisles ; *Harrold*, several rows of plain good
benches in the nave, *c.* 1600 ; *Harlington*, several rows of (*c.* 1580)
good benches at west end of nave, with buttressed ends and
moulded rails ; *Knotting*, various heavy seventeenth century
seats at west end of nave ; *Odell*, two front blocks of seats are
good seventeenth century work, enclosing backs of mediæval
seats ; *Pertenhall*, some of the pewing is *c.* 1500, and some
seventeenth century ; *Streatley*, several rows of pews—they are
exceptionally good work, *c.* 1625, heads of alternate panels are
pierced with tracery ; *Tilbrook*, some seventeenth century bench-

Stevington, Beds.

R. H. B.

Stevington, Beds.

R. H. B.

ends are used up in the modern chancel stalls ; and *Willington*, some sixteenth century carved tracery in several of the bench-ends.

BERKSHIRE

BERKSHIRE churches can show a fair amount of interesting old seats, though none of the first importance ; it may be well to take them alphabetically.   At the west end of *Aldworth*, renowned for its effigies, are some bench-ends of the days of Henry VII.   *West Challow* has some handsome fifteenth century poppy-heads.   *Childrey* has bench-ends with poppy-heads in the chancel, whilst in the south transept are several good sixteenth century seat ends, one bearing the Fettiplace arms ; here William Fettiplace founded a chantry in 1526.   At *Cumnor* the old stalls in the chancel have excellent poppy-heads.   It should be noted that the seating with poppy-heads at *Faringdon* is modern.   In the nave of *Frilsham* are some late poppy-heads. Amongst the old woodwork of the unrestored church of *West Hendred* are panels boarded up to form a vestry, some old fifteenth century benches, and some old pews, one of which has a fourteenth century end.   A certain amount of old seating was noted by us, during the 'seventies of last century, both at *Letcombe Regis* and *Lyford*.   The church of St Lawrence, *Reading*, retains some Perpendicular bench-ends.   *Sunningwell* has some exceptionally good poppy-heads on plain standards.   At *Wantage* there are eighteen stalls with misericords and poppy-heads. *Long Wittenham* possesses some poppy-head stall work brought here from the old chapel of Exeter College, Oxford, which was recklessly destroyed last century.   At *Uppington* there are many good square-headed bench-ends of early fifteenth century date.

BUCKINGHAMSHIRE

The following are the BUCKINGHAMSHIRE parish churches in possession of old seating, in alphabetical order ; some of them of primary importance, such as Haddenham, Ivinghoe, Pitstone, Stone, and Twyford.   The descriptions are chiefly taken from the Report of the *Commission on Historical Monuments* :— *Astwood.*—At the west end of the nave are four complete seats, and parts of four others with plain backs, moulded rails, and panelled standards with small buttresses ; of late fifteenth century date.   *Aylesbury.*—In addition to the stalls and misericords, there are in the chancel seven bench-ends, with traceried

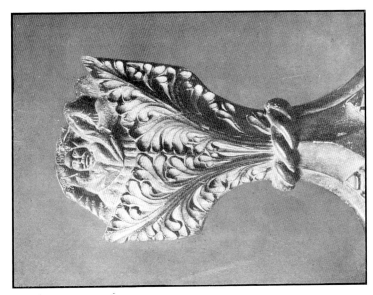

Eaton Socon, Beds.

G. C. D.

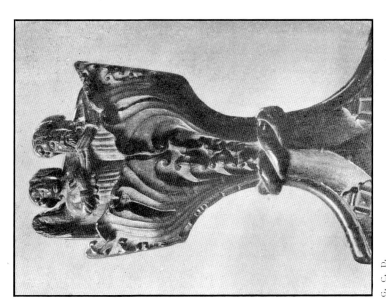

Eaton Socon, Beds.

G. C. D.

panels and poppy-heads; fifteenth century. There are six traceried heads of panels in seven standards of the seats at west end of south aisle; also the part of a seat near the south door-way with five cinquefoil open panels; also other remains of old seating in the upper vestry; all these are fifteenth century. The oak seating of the great restoration, completed in 1869, is imitative of the old work. *Brill.*—In the nave are four plain benches, possibly fourteenth century, and two small ones nearly similar in the chancel. *Buckingham.*—There are two desks at the east end of the south aisle, made up of four bench-ends with elaborately traceried panels and carved poppy-heads, fifteenth century. A third desk, made up of bench-ends with cinquefoiled panels, is dated 1626, and bears a quartered shield of Ingoldsby. In front of the gallery of the old chapel at Buckingham, of St John Baptist and St Thomas of Acton, are six bench-ends, probably brought from the parish church; they are all seventeenth century work, and bear the arms of various members of the Ingoldsby family. *Boveney.*—In the nave are eleven oak benches with shaped standards; early sixteenth century. *Chalfont St Giles.*—There are three benches in the chancel with fleur-de-lis finials, and three similar ones under the tower; probably fifteenth century. *Chesham Bois* has two benches in the chancel with moulded standards; the finials have been partly cut off, and covered with modern caps; fifteenth century work. *Chilton.*—The stalls in the chancel are made up from sixteenth century panels with traceried heads from a screen, and from two carved bench-ends with poppy-heads of the same century. *Dorney.*—In the nave are thirteen benches with plain standards; sixteenth century. *Dorton.*—The panelling round the chancel, seventeenth century, was brought here from Dorton House. *Drayton Beauchamp.*—There are five open sixteenth century benches at the west end of the nave; a sixth bench incorporates older work. *Edgcott.*—On the north side of the chancel is a standard with a small foliated finial, late fifteenth century; at the west end are five standards with trefoil finials; sixteenth century, restored. *Edlesborough.*—In addition to the six stalls, with misericords and desks in the chancel, there is under the tower the foot of a fifteenth century seat with moulded buttresses, and others of like pattern in the nave. *Grendon Underwood.*—During a restoration of 1866, some fifteenth century poppy-heads were removed from the church to the rectory, cut up, and used as ornaments! *Great Horwood.*—At the east end of the north aisle part of a fifteenth century bench-end has been incorporated with modern seating. *Great Missenden.*—The desks of the front seats in both transepts incorporate twenty-two panels with traceried heads, fifteenth century, reused from rood-screen. *Great Hampden.*— On the north side of the nave are eight old seats with linen panelled standards, and on the south side six ; early sixteenth century. *Haddenham* has a wealth of old seats of early sixteenth century date. There are eighteen in four blocks in the nave, and eleven in two blocks in each aisle. Among them are twenty original poppy-head standards, whilst some have traceried panels, two are plain, two have the rebus W and V with a tun, others have carved faces. The remaining standards are double panelled and traceried. All these seats, except the block in each aisle, have carved top rails both front and back. Lipscombe gives a good woodcut of one of these bench-ends (vol. ii., p. 214). *Hardmead.*—In the nave are six plain open seats, and in the north aisle three more, all *c.* 1580. *Haversham* has fifteen seats and two desks with rough poppy-heads ; probably late sixteenth century. *High Wycombe.*—Incorporated in the modern quire seats are eight bench-ends with poppy-heads and tracery, late fifteenth century ; removed here from the nave. *Hillesden.* —In the chancel are now two desks with linen panelled fronts, and in the nave nine seats with standards of like design ; early sixteenth century. *Horton.* — Two poppy-head standards, fifteenth century, in the chancel. *Ivinghoe* has a fine display of thirty-two poppyhead bench-ends incorporated with modern seating ; they are of fifteenth century date ; some are foliated, and some have figures and foliation. A few have been recut, whilst other poor imitations have of recent years been ejected (see Lipscombe, iii. 394-95). *North Marston.*—In addition to the six stalls in the quire, with misericords and poppy-head standards, there are in the nave a considerable number of plain old benches, apparently sixteenth century. *Monks Risborough.* —There are four poppy-head bench-ends, *c.* 1450, three carved with a small figure standing on two heads, and the fourth with two heads of women in elaborate head-dresses. *Marsh Gibbon.* —There are many early seventeenth century pews in the nave, five of which have standards with panelled sides and knob finials. *Moulsoe* has a modern litany desk formed out of early fifteenth century bench-ends. *Oving.*—At the west end of south aisle are four old benches with ornamental standards ; *c.* 1400, but restored. *Pitstone.*—The nave has nearly all sixteenth century open seats or benches, but restored. *Radclive.*—In the porch are two small benches with foliated poppy-head ends ; early fifteenth century. It is said that they have been brought here from elsewhere. *Ravenstone* has all the nave seats with shaped standards and raised back panels ; late seventeenth century. *Steeple Claydon.*—Many of the nave seats have plain shaped ends and moulded back rails ; fifteenth century, but restored. *Stoke Poges.*—At the west end of the nave is a bench, *c.* 1500, with tracery on the back, and poppy-head standards. *Stowe* seating is of interest. In the nave are five poppy-head bench-ends, reused and mounted with trefoiled panels and tracery ; sixteenth century. There are also about twenty-three heads of bench-ends reused on modern standards, also of sixteenth century date, and somewhat crude design. *Towersey.*— Four poppy-head bench-ends ; sixteenth century. *Turville.*— In the nave are five benches with moulded top rails and plain square standards, and in the vestry a bench with narrow standards ; all fifteenth century. *Twyford* seating is of much interest. In the chancel are two seats with panelled desks and standards. In the nave are twenty-two seats and desks with trefoiled standards ; the first and last standards are buttressed. In the south aisle are six other old seats or benches with standards. All are of the fifteenth century. *Willen.*—Sixteen pews in the nave have doors with raised panels, plain standards with shaped heads, and seats with moulded rails and panelled backs ; late seventeenth century. *Whitchurch.*—The standards of the chancel stalls, with rich tracery and poppy-heads, have shields with two mullets and pastoral staff in pale between the initials R. H. These stand for Robert Hobbes, Abbot of Woburn, 1529-38. *Upper Winchendon.*—At the west end of the nave are nine old benches of sixteenth century date. *Lower Winchendon.*—In the nave are ten early sixteenth century benches, but the ends are modern. *Wing.*—The greater part of the nave seating is of plain fifteenth century character, but it has been much restored and renewed. *Worminghall.*—The west half of the nave has several old benches with plain panelled standards ; late sixteenth century.

CAMBRIDGESHIRE

Considering its size, CAMBRIDGESHIRE has a fair number of surviving mediæval fittings. In twenty-eight places old quire stalls are extant, whilst ancient poppy-heads can be studied in sixteen churches. At *Babraham* there are some good fifteenth century benches in the body of the church. Twenty-six good stalls with misericords were placed in the chancel of *Balsham* towards the close of the fourteenth century by Rector Sleford, a man of great distinction ; he died in 1401. The nave of *Barrington* is fitted with well-carved fifteenth century benches.

G. C. B.

Swavesey, Cambs.

Chesterton, Cambs.

J. F. E.

Bourn has some good late stall-work, with curious poppy-heads, one of which bears the initials of " H. P. of B. A.," and the date 1534 ; in the nave are some good benches with panelled tracery, singularly like those of Carburton.   At *Burwell* there are richly carved benches both in chancel and nave ; they are probably of the same date as the lower half of the original screen, namely, 1464.   There are some carved stalls at *Caldecot*, and some remains of old open seats in the nave.   The beautiful church of *Cherry Hinton* has various old stalls and benches, with some quaintly carved poppy-heads.   *Chesterton* retains some fifteenth century benches in the chancel, with richly carved poppy-heads ; one of the most remarkable of them, crowned by a standing human figure, is here represented. These benches are absurdly said by Kelly and others to be of chestnut wood, but of course they are oak (57).   The old benches, with poppy-heads, of *Chippenham* date from about the midst of the fifteenth century.   At *Coveney*, near Ely, there is a good deal of imported foreign woodwork, but it is satisfactory to notice some good old English benches, with quaintly carved poppy-heads ; their date is *c.* 1400.   *Elsworth* has some fine re-turned stalls, with good poppy-heads ; they are noteworthy for little lockers under the book-rests or desks, with hinges and locks complete.   Though usually described as fourteenth century, the panelled linenfold backs prove them to be fifteenth century work.   Some open carved benches of the nave are of the same century.   At *Great Eversden* there are some old oak benches, and two stalls with misericords.   The fifteenth century chancel stalls of *Little Eversden* came from the old chapel of Queen's College.   In *Fordham* chancel are a good set of fourteenth century misericord stalls.   *Fulbourn* has some fine fifteenth century benches with poppy-heads to the ends.   The chapel of *Jesus College, Cambridge,* used to be the quire of the conventual church of the old established nunnery of St Radegunde. The nunnery was transformed into a college by Bishop Alcock in 1491 to 1497.   The chancel, bereft of the aisle, became the college chapel ; it was handsomely fitted with new stall work, whereon the badge and crest of Alcock were often repeated. But the changes which were made in 1789 to 1792, in accordance with the egregious taste of the day, caused deal panelling to be substituted for the richly carved oak.   The discarded oak was removed to the church of *Landbeach*.   In 1849, when a fine scheme was being carried out by Mr Pugin of restoring dignity to the chapel, application was made, but in vain, to the authorities at Landbeach to return the old stall work. Pugin devised a scheme of threefold stalls after the fashion of the original ones, and embodying one or two of the old stalls which had never left the college; the standards of the highest two were enriched by seated figures of distinguished ecclesiastics and academicians. In 1878, when Landbeach was restored, a good deal of the old work, chiefly stall-ends and panels, was returned to the college. The remarkable and renowned series of stalls in the quire of *King's College* chapel are of a hybrid character. They were executed in 1533 to 1536 after a style wherein late Gothic and Renaissance strove for the mastery; the canopies were added in the time of Charles I., whilst the panelling at the back was executed by Cornelius Austin in 1865. There are six stalls with misericords, of the fifteenth century, in the chancel of *Gamlingay*. There are also some old fifteenth century stalls with good poppy-head ends in the chancel of *Harlton*. A few carved bench-ends remain at *Trumpington*, and part of the old wooden screen had been utilised in the backs of the benches. The church of *Landbeach* is chiefly noted for having given shelter, through purchase by the then rector, to the valuable woodwork so barbarously ejected from Jesus College chapel in 1787. Some of this work has been returned to Jesus College, but much still remains, including the pulpit and lectern, and fine fourteenth century stalls with misericords, two of which bear the arms of De Lisle and Arundel, Bishops of Ely of that century (see " Builder," 27th May 1848). *Littleport* has some good fifteenth century benches with poppy-head finials to the ends. *Meldreth* has re-turned stalls with poppy-heads. The oak stalls and misericords of *Milton* came from King's College chapel. There are some Perpendicular stalls with misericords both at *Orwell* and *Over*. The chancel stalls of *Little Shelford* have traceried panels with a cresting, and bear the Freville arms, *c.* 1406. In the chancel of *Soham* are ten stalls with misericords of fourteenth century date; there are also some good fifteenth century benches with poppy-headed ends. *Swaffham Bulbeck* has a wealth of old open benches, with remains of carving and poppy-heads. The seating of the church of *Swavesey* looks old throughout; the bench-ends are crowned with most quaint fifteenth century figures of birds, beasts, fish, and human heads; but only those of the north aisle are old, from which our illustration is taken; the remainder are clever imitations done in 1867 (57). At *Thriplow, Wentworth,* and *Wood Ditton* are further instances of fifteenth century benches with poppy-headed ends. The five chancel stalls of *Willingham* have been much restored.

CHESHIRE

CHESHIRE has suffered the most of any English county from the destructions of its ancient parish churches, partly from the fact that so large a proportion of them were constructed of perishable sandstone. Nowhere, too, did the unhappy spirit of drastic "restoration" set in with greater severity during the second half of the last century than in this county. The consequence is that it is almost impossible to find any seating or bench-ends of value and importance throughout Cheshire. The solitary exception is the magnificent set of canopied stalls in the fine chancel of *Nantwich*, and these are currently supposed to have been moved here from the abbey of Vale Royal (61).

When Sir Stephen Glynne visited the church of *Acton* in 1846, he noted that the chancel contained some Jacobean stalls of wood. He also noted at *Great Budworth* "several portions of fine wood carving in the pew-ends"; but all the old seating was ejected in 1871. *Shotwick*, in the Hundred of Wirral, has at the west end of the north aisle a curious old square churchwardens' pew, on which are deeply cut the names of Henry Gorvin and William Huntington, churchwardens, 1673; over it is a wooden canopy on which is carved "Robert Coxon, James Gilbert, 1769." Glynne visited *Weaverham* in 1845, and remarked: "There are several low pews with ends of the style used in the seventeenth century"; but a restoration of 1877 cleared them away. Of *West Kirby* church, Glynne wrote in 1860 that "there are some poppy-heads within"; but we believe that these disappeared in a considerable restoration of 1869-70. *Woodchurch* was visited by this itinerant ecclesiologist as late as 1868, when he noted that "the seats are of oak; some plain original standards may be still seen among them." There is a peculiarly fine and enriched fifteenth century standard in the chancel, with an elaborate poppy-head finial.

In the south aisle of *Astbury* there is some remarkably good Jacobean pewing of the year 1616-17. At *Audlem*, in 1885, the church was reseated; some of the seventeenth century carving of the old pews was worked up into the choir seats, and some linenfold panels, with two coats of arms, were utilised as wooden sedilia. There is some good late Perpendicular pewing in the north aisle of *Cheadle*; it dates from the rebuilding of the church in 1530-40. There is also some later sixteenth century substantial work in *Nether Peover* church.

The most interesting specimens, however, of oak carving now extant in Cheshire are the three armorial panels, of early

Nantwich, Cheshire

F. H. C.

Nantwich, Cheshire

F. H. C.

sixteenth century date, in the church of *Eastham*, which are exquisite specimens of the craftsmanship of the carver. It is supposed that they originally belonged to a seat of the family of Poole, of Poole Hall, who were entitled to quarter the arms of Capenhurst and Beverton. They were probably set up by Sir William Poole, who was knighted at Lille on 14th October 1513; he was High Sheriff of Cheshire in 1527-28, and died in 1535.[1]

CORNWALL

As to CORNWALL, the most characteristic feature of the interior of a fifteenth century Cornish church was the seating throughout with substantial oak benches or seats, the square-headed ends of which were invariably carved with some degree of vigorous effect and much pains. Many of the bench-ends are of local heraldry, pertaining to such families as Arundell, Roscarrock, or Pentire, whilst initial letters, or pairs of initials, are still more frequent; these all point to pre-Reformation appropriation of seats. Numerous and interesting are the benches and standards now remaining in the county. During extended visits made by the writer to the Delectable Duchy in the 'sixties and 'seventies of last century, hardly a church could be found without a considerable number, or at least some remnants, of these fifteenth or early sixteenth century bench-ends. But the work of so-called "restoration," much of which was carried out by an architect who was a member of a well-known local family, was destructive of nearly half of their delightful woodwork. Portions are still to be found in public-house or farm-house settles, and occasionally serving as side-boards or ornamental panelling in the houses of gentle folk, well-to-do tradesmen, and "captains" of mines. In one case they were to be seen serving as doors to a pigsty. Of late years many have been eagerly snapped up by collectors of old oak, and not a few have left Cornwall for the other side of the Atlantic. The more remarkable or the larger surviving numbers are noted in alphabetical order. A few instances, or those of less note, occur at Bradock, Camborne, St Columb Minor, Davidstow, St Enoder, St Eval, St Gennys, St Goran, St Kevern, St Kew, Lawhitton, Linkinhorne, St Mylor, St Newlyn, South Petherwin, Poundstock, Rame, Sheviock, and Trevalga.

---

[1] We are indebted to Mr J. Paul Ryland, F.S.A., for the courtesy of supplying us with a description of these panels, which appeared in the *Transactions of the Historic Society of Lancashire and Cheshire* for 1909.

F. R. P. S.

Launcells, Cornwall

Instances occur of the reuse of two or three old bench-ends in modern church furniture, chiefly in pulpits or seating, as at St Cubert, Forrabury (altar front), St Gwinear, St Illogen, St Just-in-Roseland, Padstow, St Probus, St Ruan-Langhorne, St Sampson, and Whitstone.

At *Altarnun* there is a wealth of carved bench-ends of early sixteenth century—St Veronica, the Five Wounds, a Fiddler ; they include a sword dance, and a jester with caps and bells (65). Under the tower of *St Austell* are a number of bench-ends carved with symbols of the Passion, IHS, a crowned M, heraldic shields, a fox preaching, etc. At *Bodmin* there are forty good ends worked up into the frontals of the nave seats and into a low screen between chancel and south chapel ; five of those in the screen show sixteenth century arabesque work. The wardens entered into a contract with Matthew More, carpenter, in 1491, to make seats like those at St Mary's, Plympton, "or better." A very bad restoration of *St Breward* in 1864 dispersed a wealth of fine bench-ends ; we have been shown a few worked up into a farm settle ; several, including symbols of the Passion, and arms of Bodmin priory and the Lower family, were gaudily repainted and gilded, and worked up into a tasteless and unmeaning reredos ; parts of others make a rude screen at the west end. Four old misericord stalls remain in the quire of *St Buryan*, but the seats are fastened down. At *Cardinham* there are a grand number of old bench-ends, seventy-one in all, of fifteenth and sixteenth century designs. *St Columb Major* has an excellent series of fifteenth century bench-ends. Some well-carved instances remain at the badly restored church of *St Ives* ; the most notable are the front panels of a chancel seat, said to have been presented by Ralph Clies, master smith. These panels bear (1) hammer, pincers, nail, and horse-shoe ; (2) hammer and anvil ; (3) two pairs of bellows ; and (4) ladle, trammers, and clefts ; whilst two others have the busts of Clies and his wife. Two stall-ends are carved with figures of St Andrew and St Peter ; above the latter is a shield bearing the words "John Peyne," and the arms of Peyne impaling Nicholl of Penrose. John Peyne, portreeve of the town, was hung in 1549, during the cruel execution of alleged insurgents. There are many old ends at *St Juliot*, carved with sacred monograms, initial letters, and coats of arms. The carved bench-ends of *Kilkhampton* form a fine series of great variety ; they include apostolic figures, heraldic coats, such as a chevron between three mermaids, a few grotesques, scroll work, and a remarkable set of symbols of the Passion ; the latter include the thirty pieces of silver, the scourge, the spear, the ladder, the

Altarnun, Cornwall

J. N.

Altarnun, Cornwall

J. N.

9

Kilkhampton, Cornwall

Kilkhampton, Cornwall

hammer and nails, and the lantern, torches, and weapons of the garden of Gethsemane (15, 66). The Clifton pews in *Landulph* church were erected by Sir Nicholas Lower of Clifton, in 1630, and bear on the panels the arms of Lower, and of twenty other cognate families. At *Laneast* there are about thirty old bench-ends, chiefly carved with symbols of the Passion, including St Peter's cock. There are Jacobean poppy-headed bench-ends in a chapel of *Lanreath*, bearing the quartered arms of Grylls and Bane, *c.* 1620 ; there are also chancel stalls of the same date. *Lansallos* has a fine set of thirty-four carved bench-ends, several of which are heraldic, others bear heads mostly in profile, whilst one displays three faces conjoined under a coronet. *Lanteglos-by-Fowey* has a fine set of late fifteenth century benches with good carved ends throughout the church ; there is also a good deal of delicate heraldic work from seventeenth century pewing, now arranged as panelling at the west end of the south aisle. The special feature of the church of *Launcells* (63, 68, 69) is the wealth of late fifteenth century bench-ends, upwards of sixty in number, bearing curious symbols of the Ascension, Resurrection, Washing of the Feet, and the Victory over Hell, in addition to the more usual ones of the Passion (see *Reliquary*, N.S., v. 42-45). *Lewannick* suffered severely from fire in 1890 ; a great number of fine old bench-ends perished ; only one survives, dated 1546, and bearing the initials T. F. *St Mawgan-in-Pyder* has upwards of forty exceptionally well-carved bench-ends of fifteenth century date, including every variety of Passion symbol. *Michaelstow* is another church with a fine and varied series of old bench-ends. At *St Minver* is a series of arabesque ends, *c.* 1535. *Morwenstow* has a large number of ends of both fifteenth and sixteenth century dates. The church of *Mullion* is justly celebrated for the number and wealth of carving of the bench-ends ; symbols of the Passion predominate, but on others occur initials, busts of monks and soldiers, and grotesques (69). *Poughill* is another church with a large and varied collection of notable ends of both fifteenth and sixteenth century dates. *Stratton* retains thirty-three of its old bench-ends. Notwithstanding a destructive restoration of *Talland* in 1849, a large and remarkable number of old bench-ends remain ; some of them have angels in the upper part holding various symbols ; others have arms emblazoned in colour, such as Beville and Grenville ; whilst the curious human faces are unusually grotesque. Another church with a large variety of well-carved ends is that of *North Tamerton* ; in addition to the oft-recurring Passion symbols, there are many pairs of initials, a woodcock, a partridge, and various grotesque heads. The interesting church

Launcells, Cornwall

Launcells, Cornwall

Mullion, Cornwall

J. N.

Launcells, Cornwall

J. N.

of *St Teath* has a large number of bench-ends removed at a poor restoration to the aisles ; they include I HC, crowned M, symbols of Passion, and several heraldic ; the chancel desks have linenfold panels, parts of destroyed screen work ; the backs of the made-up stalls have Jacobean work. *Tintagel,* of supreme interest, has certain carved stall-ends in the chancel, which were ejected from St Teath at the restoration of 1879. At the most unhappy restoration of this church in 1870-71, a wealth of bench-ends were ruthlessly destroyed, but parts of fourteen of the number were clumsily put together and painted to form a staring and meaningless reredos, which is now mercifully hidden behind hangings. The last to be named in this alphabetical arrangement is the beautifully situated church of *St Winnow,* which to our mind shelters some of the best bench-ends in the whole county ; they are thirty-three in number, and chiefly *c.* 1525, but a few are seventeenth century ; one of the most realistic is a ship in a storm. *Zennor* has a rudely carved mermaid on a bench-end ; it is engraved in vol. xxv. of the *Antiquary.*

CUMBERLAND AND WESTMORELAND

The churches of CUMBERLAND were so exposed to the constant border raids of the Scots for several centuries that the only wonder is that even a small minimum of their pre-Reformation fittings remain to the present day. So far as woodwork was concerned, it naturally perished in the flames. It is, therefore, almost vain to look for any remnants of early sittings. After the kingdoms were united, little or no attention was paid to church fabrics in the great majority of cases. The foreign vein of Puritanism under Elizabeth, and the propinquity of Scotch Presbyterianism, united to reduce the churchmanship of those counties to a very low ebb. The fluctuating successes of the Cavaliers and Roundheads in the midst of the seventeenth century had a most disastrous effect on religious life, and when peace was for a time secured, the churches remained practically empty. Then arose George Fox, the founder of the Quakers, whose anti-Church tenets made a great impression on the two counties during the latter part of the Commonwealth rule. The Restoration was not strong enough to effect any change in favour of Episcopacy.

It was not until William Nicolson was called to the bishopric of Carlisle, which he held from 1702 to 1715, that any real effort was made to secure even common decency within the church fabrics. The visitation diaries and letters of Bishop

Nicolson show an appalling state of affairs. Out of one hundred and six churches that he visited in 1703-4, seventy-seven were in disgracefully bad order, whilst fully a score were in an absolutely scandalous condition. In sixteen churches day schools were held, mostly in the chancel, and in seventeen the only seats were backless benches.

As to seats, it may be well to go into a few extracts from the bishop's diary. *Bassenthwaite*—"The altar floor is bare, very uneven and uncomely, covered only with a few loose blew slates. Mr Highmore's Seat, with a Furbalo'ed Canopy hinders the congregation from seeing the Elements Consecrated at Sacraments." *Brampton*—"In a slovenly pickle, dark, black, and ill-seated. The Quire is yet more nasty. My Lord Carlile's Seats take up more than half of the Area, and the Altar part lyes in a most deplorable condition, without rails, or even a Table of common decency." *Crosby-upon-Eden*— "The Schoolmaster teaches the Children in the Quire, where the Boyes and Girls sit on good Wainscot Benches, and write on the Communion Table." *Irthington*—"The Seats want backs." *Stapleton*—"The Quire here is most intolerably Scandalous. No Glass in the Windows . . . no Seats. The Body of the Church is in as nasty a Pickle as the Quire . . . the Seats most scurvily low." *Threlkeld*—"The Seats are mostly unbacked." *Asby* (Westmoreland)—"The Body of the Church is tolerably well seated."

The following we believe to be the only extant early sittings in the two counties : *Greystoke*—In the quire eighteen stalls with carved misericords. *Great Salkeld* — The east end is panelled with oak from Jacobean bench-ends. *Appleby St Lawrence*—There is some low stall work, fifteenth century, each side of the chancel. *Martindale*—Various good Carolean benches. *Morland*—In the chancel are the outer frames of the backs of quire stalls, quaintly carved, *c.* 1510. The interesting church of *Beetham* (Westmoreland) retains some Carolean benches.

DERBYSHIRE

Considering the small size of DERBYSHIRE, and that its extant old churches number less than a hundred, the county is well represented in ancient sittings. The church of *Crich* certainly affords the most exceptional remains of old bench work in the county. Writing in 1878 ("Churches of Derbyshire," vol. iv., 63), we said : "There is in the vestry an old oak seat, handsomely carved and of the Perpendicular period. The ends, of considerable elevation, terminate in poppy-heads, on both sides of which are carved human faces. Unless we are wrongly informed, one, if not more, of these fine old church seats found its way to the house of Chase Cliff during the restoration, and if this is the case, we venture to hope that they may be restored to God's House." The restoration here referred to was a drastic and most mischievous affair of 1861. Judging from Mr Widdows' excellent illustrations, one at least of these purloined seats, *c.* 1500, has been replaced (73). There are now in the church two of these valuable, though mutilated, benches. Of their characteristics the photographs speak far better than mere letter-press; the ends originally belonged to seats of greater length. At *Bakewell*, which was an ancient prebendal church, there are in the chancel a number of the old stalls with misericords, but much restored; their date seems to be about 1430. *Breadsall* church used to have a valuable number of massive early sixteenth century seats with effectively carved squared ends with late Perpendicular tracery. One or two of these had interesting heraldic bearings. On one was the coat of Dunne of Breadsall; on a second an amalgamated coat of Dethick and Curzon of Breadsall; whilst a third bore this amalgamated coat quartered with Illingworth. Alas! the whole of this seating, together with other priceless woodwork, was reduced to a handful of ashes by the criminal action of those infamous women—the militant suffragettes—in July 1914. Against the side walls of the chancel of *Dronfield* are two long benches or seats of old dark oak, of early fifteenth century date, with poppy-head ends of *fleur-de-lis* design. In the north aisle of *Hartshorn* church are some old seats with carving of the Elizabethan period; on one end is "1590, B. K."; another pew-end has the initials "C. W. T. S. C. W.," and a third has the arms of Meynell and Longford, with the initials and date "E. F. 1616." The church of *Longford* was unhappily repewed in 1843, previous to which date there were many old bench-ends with both arms and poppy-heads. Three of the old poppy-heads were worked up into a reading-desk. In the grand old church of *Morley* there used to be several well-carved bench-ends, of fifteenth and sixteenth century dates, amongst the clumsy pews prior to the restoration; but the majority of these have been worked up into the present open seats. At *Mugginton* there are nineteen solid oak benches of plain but excellent designs at the west end of the nave and south aisle. Against the west wall of the aisle is an inscription to the effect that: "William Jenkinson gave to this church xxxs. that made theise formes Anno Domini M.D.C." There are some fine late fifteenth century stall-ends on the south side of the chancel

Crich, Derbyshire

G. H. W.

Crich, Derbyshire

G. H. W.

10

of *Norbury*, so famed for its Fitzherbert monuments and painted glass. At *Radbourne* there is much interesting old woodwork, most or all of which came from Dale abbey. Francis Pole of Radbourne is known to have purchased the whole of that abbey's interior fittings on its dissolution. At the west end, in front of the Pole pew, are thirteen linenfold panels, with vine leaves and fruit at their heads, and each differing in design, of early sixteenth century date. Five more of these panels have been worked up to form a casing for the font. There are also several handsomely carved bench-ends in the chancel and at the west end of the aisle, of early fifteenth century date. One of these poppy-heads is of remarkable design, for it has four representations of the human head, one of which shows a skull with the lower jaw falling after a ghastly fashion. There is some good early sixteenth century re-turned stall work in the chancel of *Sawley*, and some solid oak benches of Elizabethan date in the nave. When first we knew *Tideswell's* fine church in the 'sixties of last century, there were five old stalls on each side of the chancel of a plain massive description, but only a minimum of old work now remains, and their place is taken by local modern work. Against the north wall of the north aisle of *Weston-on-Trent* runs a stone bench table, and there is another at the west end of the south aisle. One or two old bench-ends, with fourteenth century tracery, have been used up to form a reading desk (see "Sketches of the Facsimile Society," vol. iii., Plate 25).

DEVONSHIRE

DEVONSHIRE is celebrated for the number and variety of its bench-ends. They are chiefly of late fifteenth century or early sixteenth century date. Those that adjoin Cornwall are for the most part square-ended, but those that border on Somerset are not infrequently ornamented with the poppy-head finial. The first volume of the valuable *Transactions of the Exeter Diocesan Architectural Society*, 1843, contains the report of a committee advocating open seats in contradistinction to the usual closed pews. In connection therewith five good plates are given of square-ended pre-Reformation bench-ends, engraved by J. Le Keux. They include examples from Colaton-Raleigh, Doddiscombsleigh, Ottery St Mary, Braunton, Lapford, North Tawton, Colebrooke, Norwood, Atherington, and Plymtree. As in Cornwall, there are numerous heraldic bench-ends, and others bearing pairs of initials, pointing to early instances of appropriation of seats. There is not one atom of evidence extant to

Braunton, Devon

F. S.

support the oft-repeated tales as to the carved seating in the West of England, especially in Devonshire, being the work of itinerant gangs of Flemish craftsmen. Contrariwise, there is an abundance of evidence that it is strictly English and local. It may, however, be readily admitted that arabesque designs or other Renaissance patterns, which frequently occur in the neighbourhood of the once celebrated port of Bideford, though executed by natives, came from over the seas. Such designs are unknown in the old seatings of the Midlands or the North, and nearly so in East Anglia.

We now proceed to discuss most of the old seating parish by parish in alphabetical order. The nave of *Abbotsham* has a very good series of bench-ends ; among the designs are emblems of the Passion, such as the three nails, the pincers, the lantern, the reed and sponge, and the scourges ; there are also two full-length saints, the Rood, the Bourchier knot, and several ornamental initials (3). At *Alvington* there are thirteen pre-Reformation benches or seats, with well-carved ends chiefly of tracery. The church contains several instances of late Renaissance carving, as in the manorial pew and pulpit, and there are also some bench-ends with initials, the arms of Risdon, and the date 1581. The old square-headed oak bench-ends of *Ashcombe* are decidedly quaint and rather roughly executed ; they can be best judged from the illustrations. *Ashton,* so celebrated for its beautiful and painted screen work, has also some good bench-ends. One of the bench-ends at *Ashwater* displays a biretta or priest's cap, with a monogram of T. A. below it : there were several priests of the Arscott family about this date. *Atherington* has a fine series of peculiar bench-ends, especially for Devonshire ; they are elbowed and crocketed, and terminate in small poppyheads (5). *Beer Ferrers*—The bench-ends are fairly good ; some of them bear the arms of Ferrers, with a curious augmentation of five rudders in bend sinister. *High Bickington* has some good carved woodwork, including bench-ends with a pair of apostles and other figures under elaborated canopies. Some of the benches of both *North Bovey* and *Bovey Tracey* are ancient, but the ends are not remarkable. *Braunton* has some good bench-ends, several of which are a good deal mutilated. The most interesting is one with a carving of St Brannock, the patron saint; he is represented with a chalice in his left hand, and in the base is a bullock (77). The latter refers to the legend of St Brannock restoring to life the animal of a poor man which had been killed and consumed by robbers. There are a good set of bench-ends with double emblems of the Passion in each, such as the ladder and hammer, the pillar of flagellation and the

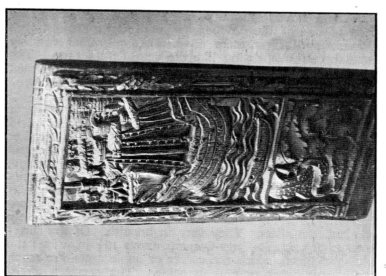

East Budleigh, Devon

F. S.

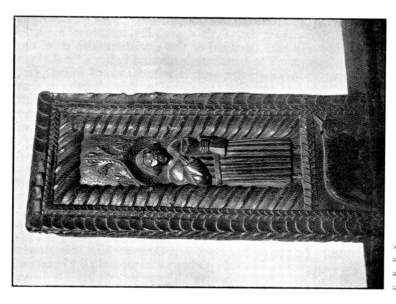

Braunton, Devon

F. R. P. S.

seamless robe, the scourge and rods, and the sponge on reed or spear. There is a handsome piece of fifteenth century carving in front of one of the old benches, with eight arcades (75). At *Broadwood Widger* there are a series of rather coarsely executed bench-ends, dating like the screen from 1529. The modern pulpit of *Buckland Brewer* has been chiefly formed out of old bench-ends. In the nave and aisles of *Buckland Monachorum* are some distinctly good carved bench-ends.

The bench-ends of *East Budleigh* amply deserve a longer treatment ; they were fully discussed by the late Dr Brushfield in vol. xxiv. (1892) of the *Devon Association*. The material of these benches or seats is exclusively oak, darkened by age, and from 3 to 4 in. thick. The backs are very slightly inclined, and, except on the bench-ends, have a continuous moulded capping. The book-boards are 5 in. and the seats 15 in. wide. The bench-ends are all square, and of the same height as the rest of the wood-work, namely, 2 ft. 11½ in. above the pew level, which is slightly raised above the aisles. They vary in breadth. Of the sixty-three remaining *in situ*, forty-five are about 16½ in. wide ; the remaining eighteen, which are corner or angle seats, are much narrower, one being only 6 in. wide. The carvings afford evidence of the date when this church was seated throughout, and this is emphasised by the exact date of 1537 inscribed on one of the bench-ends. It is generally acknowledged that the true date of the Reformation in England is 1534, so we need not be surprised to find that the whole church is destitute of a single carving in any way emblematical of the Christian faith or of the crucified Redeemer. The bench-ends abound in heraldic designs and monograms in grotesque, and in stiff forms of foliage, but it is a distinct exaggeration to describe this church, as has lately been repeatedly printed, as "a treasure-house of magnificent oak carving." A good deal of the work is distinctly poor in design when compared with other Devonshire bench-ends of earlier or even of similar date. The carving of East Budleigh has attained to great fame, firstly because of its extent, but secondly because of its intimate association with the Raleigh family, and especially with that justly famous man, Sir Walter Raleigh. The illustrations give separate special examples, numbered according to Dr Brushfield's complete catalogue. C. 4.—In the centre is a shield covered with overlapping leaves. Upon this, in the direction of a bend sinister, is a pair of broad-ended shears. In the dexter chief is a charge which it is almost impossible to describe, but it is perhaps a receptacle for heads of teasels. Below the shield is a scroll-like ornament, whilst above is a demi-angel, with wings above each shoulder. This has

East Budleigh, Devon

F. R. P. S.

East Budleigh, Devon

F. R. P. S.

been in error more than once described as a figure of Bishop Blaise, the patron saint of wool-combers, with emblems. The figure is an angel, not a saint. It was probably the seat of a well-to-do wool merchant (79). F. 8.—A half-length female figure, face in profile, looking towards the left at a large trussed bird suspended; her head covered with close-fitting cap, the gown cut low and square in front; the arms are bare to the elbow. The hands apparently lean over the half-hatch of a doorway; a platter is held in the left hand, whilst the right hand grasps the tail of a queer-looking dog on the other side of the hatch, probably intended for a turnspit (79). G. 11.—In the upper part is the vigorous representation of a ship riding on the waves. It has three masts; two of them are bare save for the rope ladders, but up the foremast a sail is being raised. Below the ship is a boat. In the upper right-hand corner the entrance to a castle is displayed. The whole character of the ship is *temp*. Henry VIII. The lower third of the panel has a squared decoration formed of convoluted leaves (77).

There are a few old bench-ends at *Christow* and *Clayhanger*. At *Cockington* there are some sixteenth century bench-ends, the panels of linenfold design. The old bench-ends at *Colaton-Raleigh* are highly exceptional, and the only ones known in the county; they are perfectly plain, with chamfered endings. There is a drawing to scale of this pre-Reformation form in vol. i. of the *Exeter Diocesan Arch. Association*. At *Colebrooke* there are considerable remains of unusual bench-ends, somewhat rudely executed; they are not square-headed, as will be seen from the two illustrations. They show the arms of Coplestone (a chevron engrailed between three leopards' faces) and of Gorges (a gorge or whirlpool), both borne by savages or wild men (81). Another end has IHC twice repeated on shields. The interesting church of *Combe-in-Teignhead* has some notable and exceptional bench-ends in the north transept. These richly carved panels are surmounted by diminutive quadrupeds; the three sides are surrounded by broad strips of foliage or flowers, the bottom corners terminating in human faces; at the base are elaborate quatrefoils, whilst each of the niched figures is surmounted by a quatrefoiled head. Two of the ends have single central figures; in the one case it is a crowned St Catherine, carrying as her emblems the wheel and a sword; the other is St Mary Magdalene, with long flowing hair and carrying the jar of spikenard. In the latter case, the marginal borders are composed of slips of single cinquefoiled flowers. The two other ends are divided into four, each with its niched figures. One of these has the figures of St Peter and St Paul above,

Colebrooke, Devon

F. S.

Colebrooke, Devon

F. S.

11

and two woodhouses or wild men below.   The other is carved
with figures of Saints George, Agnes, Genest, and Hubert.

Lapford, Devon

F. S.

Combe-in-Teignhead, Devon

E. W. A.

St Genest, who so seldom appears in any form of sacred art,
was a comedian and mimic of the days of Diocletian ; when
burlesquing Christianity on the stage, he was baptized in
derision ; but it was effectual, he openly professed the Faith, and

was martyred. This quaint figure is arrayed in fool's dress, with cap and bells (82). At *Cookbury* there are some old

Rewe, Devon

E. W. A.

Countisbury, Devon

F. S.

bench-ends curiously carved, but they have been a good deal restored. *Countisbury* church was chiefly pulled down and rebuilt in 1796; the tower was rebuilt in 1835 to 1836, and a general restoration carried out and a new north aisle built in

1846. Guide books tell us that there is nothing left of any interest in the interior. But this is by no means true, for worked up into a modern pew is an old bench-end, in the centre of which is a beautifully carved example of the Bohun badge, a swan ducally gorged ; below are the arms of Courtenay (three torteaux and a label of three points) within a quatrefoil ; above are the letters "IHS MAR" (83). *Doddiscombsleigh* has some remnants of old bench-ends, but the church was almost entirely reseated in 1887. *Downland* has several fifteenth century bench-ends, chiefly tracery with devices on shields ; at the base of one are St Peter's crossed keys. *Down St Mary* possesses some well-carved bench-ends. One of these divided into two panels has a mermaid on the dexter siding, holding a mirror in one hand and a comb in the other (87). Another double one is carved with two male heads in profile facing each other. A third, single one, has a man carrying over his shoulder a rod with three knotted thongs suspended from it. It used to be considered a ' bunch of grapes, but to our mind it is a terrible weapon for flagellation, and may have been intended as an emblem of the Passion. Both these latter are illustrated in Mr John Stubbs' "Church Antiquities in Devon," 1909. The late fifteenth century bench-ends of *Frithelstock* are a good series ; they include the crowned double rose of Henry VII., a single feather with label for Henry, Prince of Wales, the arms of Hartland abbey, a stag's head impaled with a crosier, and divers other figures and emblems. The bench-ends of *Harpford* display on shields the initials " M. B.," " W. I.," and " T. D. " ; the last may possibly refer to one of the Drake family, who were once resident in this parish. The nave of the fine church of *Hartland* is chiefly fitted with substantial benches of late sixteenth century date. In the south chapel are several bench-ends bearing the initials " H. P." ; they stand for Hugh Prust. He was a leading landowner of Hartland, and the last upholder of the Guild of Our Lady before the Reformation ; these seats have been transferred from the old Lady chapel to the other side of the church. At the fine old cruciform church of *Holbeton* there are modern bench-ends, designed by Mr Sedding (*frontispiece*) (85). The church of *Horwood* was restored in 1889, when some old bench-ends were utilised in forming a reading-desk. At *Ilsington* there is a fine richly carved series of bench-ends, with poppy-heads, such an exceptional feature in Devonshire churches ; on them may be noted the arms of Beaumont and Pomeroy, who were the chief landowners of the parish in the thirteenth century. These bench-ends are probably the earliest in the county. There are canopied

F. H. C.

Holbeton, Devon

seats in the north chancel. The church of *Kenn*, to the east of Exeter, contains a few bench-ends. Some of the good *Landcross* bench-ends have been worked up to form a modern pulpit, a use which has also been followed at the neighbouring church of Buckland Brewer. There are, however, other noteworthy Landcross bench-ends with a great diversity of design, including emblems of the Passion, and shields bearing monograms or initial letters. *Lew Trenchard* has a few somewhat remarkable bench-ends. One of them in the north aisle has a vigorous St Michael weighing souls; the heads peeping out of the tops of the scales are decidedly quaint. This end is illustrated by Mr Stubbs in his "Church Antiquities of Devon." One represents the embattled gateway of a castle, with a curious bearded man's head above it; a narrow one has a full length saint with right hand raised in blessing, and a ball resting in the left hand; the third, with a bust above, has a quaint figure below, possibly intended for St Genest, the jester saint. *Littleham*, near Bideford, has several old bench-ends, late in Henry VIII.'s reign, incorporated with the new seats. The treatment is obviously Renaissance. Here and elsewhere near the port of Bideford dolphin-like ornaments occur. The dolphin was the badge of the Dauphin; the Renaissance reached France some little time before it crossed the Channel. These designs were probably copied from those of French origin. The arms and crests, with a crescent for difference, are those of St John. In the south or Annery aisle of *Monkleigh* church are some very good bench-ends. The emblems of the Passion include lantern, cock, reed and sponge, hammer, ladder, scourge, hand holding a bag, thirty pieces of silver, cross, and crown of thorns. One of the bench-ends bears the date 1508. *Lapford* has a remarkable and varied series of bench-ends. One of them is quite early in the fifteenth century, and possibly towards the close of the fourteenth century; it has stiff squared foliage, and note also the plain rounded mouldings of the top and sides (87). The rest are mostly of the days of Henry VIII., and several of them have distinctly Renaissance designs (89). One of them represents a man with a terrible instrument of flagellation, like one at Down St Mary (82). In several cases there are initials such as "S. I.," which undoubtedly stand for St John, a noted family of this parish. Perhaps the most interesting are three pairs of heads in profile, of which one is here illustrated (89); they are shown in profile, male and female facing each other. Is it not possible that they were intended to be portraits of the respective owners of the seats? The headgear varies in each. One of the smaller ends shows the Five Wounds. At *North*

Lapford, Devon

F. S.

Down St Mary, Devon

F. S.

Lew there are many old bench-ends, but they were over-repaired during a disastrous restoration of 1885. One of them is dated 1537, and this is probably the approximate date of the whole; it is the same date as the yet larger collection at East Budleigh. They exhibit various heraldic badges, and the arms of several county families. A single elaborate heraldic end, near the priest's door, illustrated by Mr Stubbs, is thus described by Mr Hamilton Rogers in his "Sepulchral Effigies of North Devon":—"(1) St Ledger; (2) or, a chief indented azure (Butler, Earl of Ormond); (3) a lion rampant (Rochford); (4) Hankford; (5) Stapledon; (6) three pairs of pincers (Donet); above, a helmet with crest, on a wreath a falcon rising from a panache of ostrich feathers (Butler); supporters, dexter, a falcon; sinister, a griffin." At a restoration of *Newton St Petrock* in 1884, the pews were removed, and the old work of some fifteenth century benches was included in the new scheme of open seating. Some of the old benches have been made up into a pulpit, the panels being emblems of the Passion. *Northleigh* has some effectively carved bench-ends. The panel illustrated shows floral designs divided by a saltire cross. In the old episcopal church of St James of *Okehampton*, rebuilt in 1862, a few old bench-ends are, we believe, still extant. *Ottery St Mary*—This splendid and nobly proportioned church has a wealth of interesting woodwork. The old bench-ends are noteworthy; the design of a vase from which spring cinque-foiled flowers is specially effective, and the double Tudor vase of Henry VII. is a vigorous piece of carving. Illustrations appeared in the *Builder* of 5th January 1907. There are also a few old bench-ends at *Peyhembury* and at the small cruciform church of *West Putford*, so seldom visited; they also may be noted at *Feniton* and *Talaton*. At *Plympton St Mary* are some carved benches and bench-ends; one of these displays eight shields illustrating the alliances between the Strodes and Courtenays. One of the *Plymtree* bench-ends has a shield bearing a merchant's mark intertwined with a letter "G"; it refers to Thomas Goodwyn, a former landowner of this parish. At *Rewe* there are some interesting bench-ends and other good work; some of these ends bear shields of Wadham impaling Seymour and Chiselden. The one here illustrated (83) has an effective traceried design, with the names "George, Col, and Jone . . .," to whom this seat was doubtless appropriated. There are some very good bench-ends in the ancient church of *Sutcombe*, richly carved, chiefly heraldic. There are a variety of loose ones at the west end of the north aisle, the remnants of a somewhat hasty restoration. Three bear shields of the Prideaux

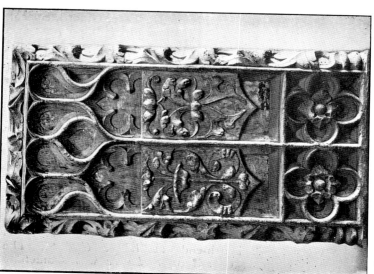

Lapford, Devon

F. S.

Lapford, Devon

F. S.

family, one is of six quarterings, whilst several have various initials. There are also shields of De Esse, Gifford, Spacot, Dennis, Wyke, and Spencer. Amongst other designs are two fish, a merman and mermaid, a St Andrew's Cross, a double knot, various beasts and dragons with convoluted tails, and two full-length figures, perhaps intended for Apostles. There are also various symbols of the Passion on the restored stalls within the chancel screen. In *Seaton* church there are a few fifteenth century panels left, but it was badly treated under restoration, when it lost several good bench-ends. The bench-ends of *Tavistock* are chiefly copies of the originals. *Tawstock* has some very good bench-ends, as also *Torrington* and *North Tawton*; those of *Thorverton* have heraldic shields. There are others at the small church of *Venn Ottery*. "Cart-loads of old carved benches were removed and destroyed, to be replaced by deal," from the church of *Virginstow*, when it was rebuilt in 1852, says Mr Baring Gould; a few fifteenth century ones remain, including one with the initials "B. D." There are some good examples of heraldic bench-ends at *Weare Giffard*. The ancient little cruciform church of *Welcombe* was shamefully treated at the restoration of 1883 to 1884. It used to possess some highly interesting and exceptional poppy-heads (of which we took notes in the 'seventies), but they have been sawn off, and the mutilated bench-ends patched up to form the base panels of a beautiful and much later screen. *Woolfardisworthy*, near Bideford, possesses a few good bench-ends.

DORSETSHIRE

DORSETSHIRE has but sparse remnants of the ancient seating. "The lovable village church" of *Affpuddle*, as Sir Frederick Treves justly calls it, has a fine series of well-carved bench-ends with good poppy-head finials of sixteenth century date. One of them bears this inscription in bold lettering:—"Thes seatys were mayd in the yere of our Lord God MCCCCCXLVIII, the tyme of Thomas Lyllington, vicar of thys church" (91). The back of the westernmost seat on the south side has good linenfold panels. The pew-ends of *Bere Regis* church show some good carving of the sixteenth century; one is dated 1547, and another bears the name of "ION. DAY. WARDEN. OF. THIS. CHARYS" (*sic*). At *Bradford Abbas* the ends of many of the pews are richly carved with floriated foliage; they mostly terminate in poppy-heads, and two of them have little animals on the elbows. On the one by the font is a well-executed pig

F. H. C.   Trent, Dorset

C. F. N.   Affpuddle, Dorset

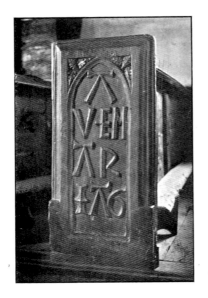

E. W. W.

Trent, Dorset

feeding on the mast under an oak, with birds among the branches. A square-topped end bears St Paul with sword and book. The grand quire of *Sherborne abbey* church has been lavishly restored during recent years; the finely carved desk-ends of the stalls are, we believe, modern work, as well as the canopies over the seats, but the seats themselves and the misericords are old. *Trent* (recently transferred from Somerset to Dorset) has two blocks of sixteenth century bench seats. Two of the bench-ends bear the words *Ave Maria*. The figure depicted on another one is probably intended for St John with the poisoned chalice (91); a second one bears a stag in a curious upright position; and a third has a singular arrangement of emblems of the Passion. At *Toney Puddle* there are some beautiful sixteenth century square-backed bench-ends covered with arabesque tracery. *Yetminster* retains many of its ancient low oak benches, capped with Tudor flowers, *c.* 1500.

DURHAM

Though small in amount, there is much interest pertaining to the surviving old seating of the county of DURHAM. The thirty-two Bishop Cosin stalls of the cathedral have been noticed elsewhere. The fittings at *Aycliffe* are quaint and characteristic throughout. They are certainly seventeenth century, and are usually spoken of as "Jacobean," that vague and misleading term; they seem to us undoubtedly post-Restoration. Surtees tells us that in his days (1779-1834) there was a screen between nave and chancel bearing the arms of Charles I., and that the stall and desks of the church showed considerable taste. The pews of comparatively modern height have open rails at the top like some at *St Helens, Auckland,* and *Staindrop.* The seats have since been altered, and their backs made to slope to suit modern ideas of comfort. The richly carved chancel screen of the fine church of *Brancepeth,* together with the quire stalls, the pulpit, and the series of panelled seats with carved ends in the body of the church, are all the work of John Cosin, rector from 1636 to 1644, and afterwards the celebrated Bishop of Durham (31,94). In the chancel of *Coniscliffe* are some fifteenth century stalls and desks, having standards with angels' busts as finials. The massive stalls of the quire of the great church of *Darlington* show the arms of Thomas Langley, cardinal, and Bishop of Durham 1406 to 1438, and his eagle badge; as to the interesting misericords, see Mr Bond's volume on that subject. In the chapel of *Durham Castle* there are twenty-two

C. B. S.

Brancepeth, Durham

Durham Castle

W. M.

Durham Castle

W. M.

stalls, *c.* 1510, but only eleven of them retain their misericords. They were brought here in 1547 from the upper chapel of Bishop Auckland, and are chiefly remarkable for the four exceptionally fine standards or bench-ends, worked under Bishop Ruthall (1508-23), with fine poppy-headed finials. One of them is carved with good late Perpendicular tracery. Another one bears the arms of the See of Durham, a cross patonce between four lions rampant. A third carries the arms of the See impaling those of Ruthall, a cross between four doves, in chief three roses slipped. The fourth has this last impaled coat exactly reversed; it seems obvious that the carver mistakenly worked from the matrix of the episcopal seal, instead of from an impression (95). The late fifteenth century chancel stalls of *St Oswald's, Durham,* are distinctly good; there is also a remarkable double sedilia of wood, well carved, *c.* 1400. *Easington* church has an abundance of benches, the ends of which are carved with ornamental foliage and fruit, pendant by ribbons from the tops, which terminate in foliated poppy-heads. There has been much difference of opinion as to the date of the carving of these exceptional bench-ends, but probably they are not later than 1634 ("Arch. Ael.," xvii.). Four of the various seventeenth century bench-ends of *Gateshead* bear arms; two of them, incorporated into the reading-desk, show the arms of Cole, and of Riddell impaling Tonge; in the north transept is a bench-end bearing Riddell, and in the south transept is a fourth bearing Halls. The interesting church of *Haughton-le-Skerne* is filled with oak stalls and pews which date from about the Restoration; when this church was about to be restored in 1870, it was resolved by the committee: "That the whole of the oak fittings being not only very handsome and elaborate in themselves, but of the highest ecclesiastical interest, should be strictly preserved throughout; such repairs or reseating only being undertaken as may be found absolutely necessary." *Heighington* has three or four old benches in the chancel, tower, and vestry; the standards finished with diamond-shaped poppy-heads, and the projecting part of the seats (which are wider than the standards) supported at each end by turned little balusters; they are late Elizabethan or early Jacobean. In the chancel of *Jarrow* are four bench-ends with elaborate well-carved and traceried sides of late fifteenth century date. One of the finials bears the well-known badge of Prior Thomas Castel (1494-1519), a winged heart pierced by an arrow (97). At *Lanchester* there is some post-Reformation stall work; it is figured in the "John O'Gaunt Sketch Book," ii. 16. *Sedgefield* has some good canopied stalls in the chancel of seventeenth century date. At

W. M.

Jarrow

the hospital chapel of *Sherburn* are sixteen stalls of the same century. Some similar stall work is also to be noted at *Staindrop* and *Stanhope*, which is Gothic in character though post-Reformation.

ESSEX

ESSEX is fairly well represented in pre-Reformation seating, and the following are the instances which we have personally noticed.

There is good stall work at *Belchamp St Paul*, ten stalls with misericords or poppy-headed ends ; at *Castle Hedingham* the stalls have grotesque carving ; also some old stalls at *Newport*. At *Shalford* there is a single stall, known as "the Abbot's Chair," with particularly good poppy-heads (99).

As to old benches or standards, they are sufficiently numerous to be briefly mentioned in alphabetical order. In the south aisle of *Great Burstead* there is a range of old fifteenth century benches with traceried ends. *Great Clacton* has a few good old benches, but most of the oak sitting only dates from a restoration of 1865. At *Danbury* there are three old poppy-headed bench-ends, with small figures on the elbows ; there are also some tracery-headed panels let into the front of a pew, but these probably formed part of the rood-screen. A few fifteenth century benches remain at the west end of the nave of *Epping Upland*, with poppy-head finials to the standards. The oak benches of the nave of *Fairstead* are of early sixteenth century date ; the ends are carved with the linenfold pattern. Of the same date and style are some old benches at *Little Leigh* ; but the ends and backs of some of the benches at *Great Leigh* are early fifteenth century. At *Liston* a single old poppy-headed bench remains. There is some old benching in the very small church of *Norton Mandeville*. At *Rettendon* there are some good early fifteenth century benches in the chancel, with notable poppy-head finials, one of which is carved with the Bear and Ragged Staff, and another with the Stanley Eagle and Child (99). At the west end of the north aisle of *Stock* are four good fifteenth century benches with poppy-head ends and small figures on the elbows. At *Takeley* are several old bench-ends with well-carved tracery. Some ancient benches also remain at *Great Tey*. The fine large church of *Thaxted* has various portions of old seating. There are, or were in 1905, certain fragments of the quire stalls at the west end ; some good fifteenth century pewing with buttressed panels, having good traceried

F. R. T.

Shalford, Essex

T. M. G. L.

Rettendon, Essex

heads, and quatrefoils at the base; adjacent to these are several tall standards well carved with early sixteenth century designs (100). At *Great Waltham* many of the late fifteenth century benches are retained with good traceried ends. *Wendens Ambo* is remarkable for some old pews in the chancel which have curious corner posts with animals on the summit; on one of these is the ugly figure of a hyena grinning in a mirror, cut out of the solid beam or post. At *West Hanningfield* are some old benches, whilst at *Woodham Ferrers* and *Writtle* there are several with poppy-head finials.

A. W. A.

Thaxted, Essex

GLOUCESTERSHIRE

Though GLOUCESTER-SHIRE is more or less of a paradise to the enthusiastic ecclesiologist, it is by no means pre-eminent in its remains of old seating, providing always that we except the stall work at the two cathedrals of Bristol and Gloucester, the former of which are canopied, *c.* 1520, and the latter, sixty-two in number, *c.* 1560, with ogee canopies, together with the fourteenth century stalls of *Tewkesbury* and the fifteenth century stalls of *Fairford*. In *Aust* church there is an old oak chair popularly supposed to have been used by Wicliff, an idea that has more than once found its way into print; but Wicliff died in 1384, and the chair is of seventeenth century date. Moreover, there is no ground for the current notion that Wicliff ever preached within this fabric. In the north aisle of *Blaisdon* are some of the old fifteenth century seats with carved bench-ends. At *Bledington* there are fifteenth century bench-ends to the pews throughout the church, but inserted as panels. *Buckland*

Winchester Cathedral

has a large number of fifteenth century benches. At *Churchdown* there are some good fifteenth century bench-ends, with central finials and curved sides (see "Spring Gardens' Sketch Book," vol. i., Plate 5). *Didbrook* has Laudian altar rails ; the oak seats are also probably Carolean. There are four misericord stalls on the south side of the quire of *Duntisbourne Rous*. The quire stalls of far-famed *Fairford* have quaint misericords, *c.* 1460. The church of *St Mary-de-Lode*, *Gloucester*, has some good carved benches of the Perpendicular period. There are also some old carved bench-ends at *Hasfield*. The small church of *Hill* has some fourteenth century oak benches. *Iron Acton* has many buttressed seat-ends, *c.* 1580, with linenfold panels, narrowed for the fronts of the seats, but wider for the standards ; there are six of these linenfold panels buttressed to the back seats next the cross passage (see "Spring Gardens' Sketch Book," vol. vii., Plates 23, 24). At *Lower Lemington* there is a chair constructed out of old bench-ends. *Notgrove* has some well-carved old pewing of late fifteenth century date ; on the back of the reading pew is " Richard de Noel and Thomas de Noel, Churchwardens, 1619." In the quire of *Sapperton* are two pews of old linenfold panels, and two fronts to stalls of like design under the tower, *temp.* Henry VIII. ; there is also much elaborate woodwork, *temp.* Queen Anne. Both *Stoke Orchard* and *Tredington* have Elizabethan benches.

HAMPSHIRE

HAMPSHIRE, though of considerable size and possessing a multiplicity of churches, has a comparative scarcity of ancient seating. The remarkably fine stalls of *Winchester Cathedral* (68 stalls, *c.* 1296, and *Christchurch*, 58 stalls) have already received attention in previous volumes of this series. In the north quire of *Alton* there are some fifteenth century old stalls with misericords. The south aisle of *Bentworth* has some plain oak benches of the sixteenth century. At *Bramley* some of the old seats with buttressed bench-ends, *c.* 1500, remain. *Chilbolton* has sixteenth century linenfold panels in part of the quire seats facing east. In the nave of *Empshott* are a good number of benches, *c.* 1600, with trefoiled panels in the standards. At *Heckfield* there are some remains of old benches. The chancel of *Monk's Sherborne* has some good solid oak benches of fifteenth century date with poppy-headed finials to the standards. The great galleries of *Odiham*, erected in 1638 at the west end of the aisles, are furnished with their original sittings. The timber-paved fifteenth century nave of *Rotherwick* retains the original plain benches with roll-moulded tops. The stalls and other woodwork of *Romsey* abbey are all modern. The quire of the fine church of the hospital of *St Cross*, Winchester, is supplied with curious cinquecento stalls carved with the date 1570. At *Selborne* there are a few old benches at the west end, and two in the porch with ends panelled in trefoiled arches, all of late fifteenth century date. The seating of *Timsbury* includes a number of old plain benches. Only one standard remains perfect; it has two circular finials; we believe the date to be late thirteenth century. In the nave of *Titchborne* are some good seventeenth century pews, with the Titchborne arms on that at the south-east. The benches of the nave

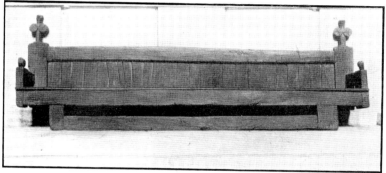

G. C. D.

Winchester Cathedral

of *Warnford* are plain and massive; they date towards the close of the sixteenth century. The best feature of that extraordinarily attractive house in Sherborne St John, begun early in the sixteenth century by William, Lord Sandys, and known as *The Vyne*, is undoubtedly the chapel. It contains most of the original and exquisitely carved fittings, having exquisitely carved canopied seats on north and south, and re-turned on the west; the fronts are panelled with tracery in the heads, whilst the standards are beautifully treated and crowned with elaborate poppy-headed finials. Nor must it be forgotten that the south transept of *Winchester* cathedral has an early detached bench of somewhat rude but strong construction; it is sometimes claimed to be Norman, but we do not believe it to be earlier than the second half of the thirteenth century (103). There is much fine woodwork (restored) in the Lady chapel of the cathedral (101).

HEREFORDSHIRE

The remains of mediæval church seatings are but few in HEREFORDSHIRE, and those that are extant are chiefly stall work in the quires. The unhappy rage for restoration and uniformity of last century is responsible for sweeping away much that represented the best art and craftsmanship of different generations of our forefathers. When we read that the old church of *Aymestrey*, as long ago as 1804-6, was "reseated in oak from the

G. C. D.

Garway, Herefordshire

materials of the old benches," it can be at once realised how much more desirable it was in its older garb. *Bishop's Frome* lost many ancient benches as the result of a restoration in 1861, and *Bosbury* was "repewed" by Mr Christian, that sadly iconoclastic architect, in 1871. *Coddington* experienced a like treatment in 1866. Contrariwise, *Clodock* still remains seated with fifteenth century benches. *Canon Pyon* shelters in its chancel sixteen stalls with their misericords; a very possible tradition has it that these stalls were rescued from Wormesley priory on its dissolution in the evil days of Henry VIII. Parts of the old pewing of *Eaton Bishop* were used up in the seats at the west end during a restoration of 1899. At *Garway* there are a few old benches, the standards of which, as will be seen from the plate (104), are peculiarly rude and early ; the curved outline of their tops appears to represent the earliest dawn of the poppy-head ; we are inclined to date them towards the close of the thirteenth century. The richness of the canopied stalls of *Hereford* cathedral has been already treated in a previous volume of this series. In the same city are the eight stalls under a continuous coved canopy at *St Peter's*, of fifteenth century date, but restored ; and the beautiful canopied stalls of *All Saints*, said to have been used by the brethren of St Anthony's Hospital. At *Kimbolton* the chancel was provided with stalls in 1873, constructed out of sixteenth century pewing which was destroyed for that purpose. *Lingen*, rebuilt in 1890, retains the old benches which were brought here from the neighbouring destroyed church of Deerfold, a building which suffered severely in the Civil War. At *Ledbury* there are nine stalls with misericords and desks. There are also some surviving stalls at *Madley*. *Wigmore*, formerly attached to the wealthy abbey of Austin canons, retains some good stall work.

HERTFORDSHIRE

The county of HERTFORD has some good remains of old quire stalls and several benches, but nothing very remarkable. It will be seen from the following notes that poppy-heads occur in eight churches.

Anstey has twelve early fourteenth century stalls ; there are seven Renaissance, but only three are original ; the stall fronts are seventeenth century. At *Ardeley* there are open seats of the fifteenth century with poppy-head finials. In the nave of *Bonington* are some fourteenth century benches. *Bishop Stortford* has eighteen quire stalls with misericords ; the backs are traceried, the fronts panelled, and the standards have poppy-heads ; the whole fifteenth century. At *Braughing* there are a few buttressed bench-ends in the nave, of early sixteenth century date. The nave of *Caldecote* has some plain fifteenth century benches. *Clothall* has some poppy-headed fourteenth century bench-ends. At the end of the south aisle of *Flamstead* there is some late fourteenth century seating. At *Hitchin*, behind the screens of the south chapel, are remains of the stalls for the Fraternity of the Guild of Our Lady, founded *temp.* Edward IV., with short seats facing east, like those at Newark. In the chancel of *Kimpton* there are six poppy-headed bench-ends

14

of the fifteenth century. The nave of *Knebworth* is furnished throughout with moulded fifteenth century benches. Many of the seats of *Laystone* are fifteenth century. The quire seats of *Little Gaddesden* have poppy-headed standards, and front panelling of the seventeenth century. At *Little Hadham* there is some panelling in the north transept, taken from seventeenth century pewing. *Much Hadham* has some fifteenth century quire stalls. The oak stalls in the chancel of *Great Munden* bear the initials " R.K."; Richard King was rector 1516-38; they are sadly disfigured by paint. The plain seating in the nave of *Norton*, with moulded rails, is *c.* 1550. The nave of the church of *St Michael's*, *St Albans*, has much linenfold panelling, *c.* 1500, worked up in the seating. There are some poppy-headed bench-ends at the west end of the nave of *Sandon.* In the nave of *Sawbridgeworth* are several early fourteenth century benches, with square-headed linenfold bench-ends. The modern seating of *Shenley* has some old carved poppy-heads. *Stevenage* has three stalls, with misericords in the chancel, and three more under the tower; date *c.* 1400. The seating in the nave of *Throcking* is almost all seventeenth century; but in the chancel is a single bench-end with a poppy-head carved with three human figures and a bird. In the nave of *Wallington* are several plain mediæval benches. In the chancel of *Westmill* are seats with early sixteenth century standards; in the aisle are several benches with buttressed ends and moulded rails, *c.* 1580. In the north transept of *Wheathampstead* are two seats dated 1631; they were brought here from Lamer Park chapel. There are late fifteenth century stalls in the chancel of *Willian*, the standards of which have carved bench-ends, one of which represents an elephant, and another the head of St John Baptist in a charger. In the aisle of *Wyddial* are four pews of the same date as the screen, namely, early seventeenth century; they are handsomely carved in the top panels.

HUNTINGDON

The small county of HUNTINGDON is nearly akin to its neighbour of Northampton in the beauty of its churches; there is a fair amount of interest in the revival of its ancient fittings, though the rage for uniformity destroyed much during the last century. The reckless way in which early restorers treated old seatings is well illustrated in the case of *Alwalton.* A writer in the "Gentleman's Magazine" for 1842 says of their ancient church : " It had been disfigured by every enormity, by pews, or rather

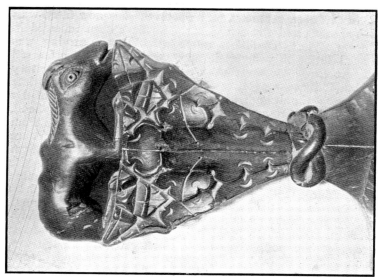

Eynesbury, Hunts.

G. C. D.

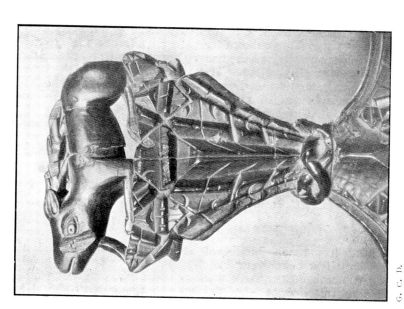

Eynesbury, Hunts.

G. C. D.

cribs, of every shape, size, height, and colour . . . All these defects have been removed. The body of it is now fitted with open free seats, and the remaining pews have been renewed in a uniform style." Doubtless much valuable old carving was destroyed during this wholesale process. *Barham* has a few old seats. At *Brampton* there used to be three fourteenth century stalls, but it has, strangely enough, been thought fit to translate them to the Cambridge Museum. In the possession of Dr Philip Nelson is a remarkably good and interesting poppy-head, *c.* 1500, with two demi-angels bearing shields. It came from the palace of the Bishops of Lincoln at *Buckden* ; the arms are a chevron between three roses, which were borne by William Smith, a co-founder of Brasenose College ; he held the bishopric from 1496 till 1514. *Diddington* has some fine Perpendicular panelling in connection with former stall work ; the spandrels of the tracery are most cunningly carved. *Eynesbury* has a large number (thirty-two) of quaint poppy-heads rising from old standards of late fifteenth century date ; the tops of the poppy-heads spread out widely at the top, and on the summit are some grotesque quadrupeds (107). *Fen Stanton* has some good open seats. In the post-Reformation small church of *Little Gidding*, where that remarkable man, Nicholas Ferrar, founded a little community soon after 1625, the seats are arranged facing each other as in a collegiate chapel. *Great Gransden* has some good buttressed panelling of the fifteenth century as a pew front ; the artistic carving in the spandrels of the tracery appears to be by the same craftsman as at Diddington. There are some seats in the rear of *Glatton* with finely carved poppy-heads ; they were illustrated in the " Penny Post " of 11th February 1883. There are a few old benches at *Godmanchester, Hamerton,* and *Offord Cluny,* all apparently of the fifteenth century. At *Great Paxton* there are benches, late in the same century, with square-topped and buttressed standards, and rounded mouldings. *Little Paxton* has some stalls with misericords. *Southoe* has some old open benches, the standards of which terminate in poppy-heads.

KENT

KENT has much mediæval stall work remaining, but surprisingly few benches or bench-ends. There is some good carved fifteenth century oak work at *Aldington,* including six stalls with misericords. At *Ashford* the upper row of stalls with misericords are original. An old poppy-head bench-end,

E. W. A.

East Barming, Kent

of an ordinary fifteenth century type, remains at *Bapchild.*
East Barming has some curious bench-end carving, including
Our Lord delivering souls from prison, and St Michael slaying
the dragon, which is described in Mr Bond's " Dedications,

Saints, and Emblems," page 274. *Bethersden* lost many of its old fifteenth century benches in 1851. *Bexley* church was restored in 1803 ; various fragments of fifteenth century seats were preserved in the repairing ; they were used as models for the present buttressed ends or standards. Sir Stephen Glynne, in 1846, commented on Bexley's "frightful pews." He found inscribed on one set : " These three pews built at charge of the parish 1765." The church of *Bidborough* was reseated in 1894, but some good old poppy-headed bench-ends and benches were retained. *Cliffe-at-Hoo* has six stalls with misericords. *Cobham*, so renowned for its brasses, retains some stall work in its collegiate chancel with a single misericord on the south side ; much damage was done to this seating during a miserable restoration of 1860. Of *North Cray*, in 1849, Glynne wrote : " The chancel is sadly encumbered with pews quite close to the altar ; the nave also abounds with pews, some of which are embellished with rich carving." A panel with a Renaissance canopy, *c.* 1530, is illustrated in Mr Bond's " Emblems of Saints." In the quire of the capacious church of *Faversham* are twelve old stalls ; there are also fifteenth century quire stalls at *Ivychurch* and *Lenham*. *High Halden*, restored by Street in 1868, has quire stalls modelled from some old work pertaining to a long narrow pew in the south-west corner of the unrestored chancel. The quire of *Maidstone* retains twenty-six canopied stalls with misericords, placed there in 1395-96 ; there are ten on each side, and six facing east. *West Malling* has some interesting stall work. The chancel of *Minster-in-Thanet* has a noble set of early fifteenth century stalls with misericords ; they are eighteen in all, ten on the north side and eight on the south. On one on the north side is the name of Johannes Curteys, who was rector from 1401 to 1419. The stall-ends, with poppy-head finials, are all different ; one of the finest, with Perpendicular tracery, was engraved in the "Builder" during 1845. *Preston-next-Faversham* has two fifteenth century benches in the chancel ; the standards have poppy-head finials. In the chancel of *Rodmersham* are three wooden sedilia with canopies. There are some good fifteenth century stalls with misericords in the chancel of St Clement's, *Sandwich*. Sir Stephen Glynne noted in *Southfleet* church, " many remnants of ancient stalls and carved pew ends." At *Thorley* there are four stalls, *c.* 1450. Archbishop Peckham founded a collegiate establishment at *Wingham* in 1280 ; the stalls with misericords are still all extant.

Halsall, Lancashire

G. G. E.

LANCASHIRE

LANCASHIRE, notwithstanding the renewal of so many of her churches, has some interesting remains of old seating of various dates. *Blackburn.*—The church of St Mary was entirely rebuilt between 1820 and 1826. Under the tower of the new church are eight old oak stalls with misericords. In the galleries are preserved a number of old benches about 6 ft. long, with shaped graded ends of sixteenth century date, and there is also one in each porch. *Bolton-le-Moor.*—The old church of St Peter was rebuilt in 1867-71. Fine carved bench-ends of fifteenth century date are preserved in the quasi-museum in the tower basement of the new church. *Cartmell* priory church, so renowned for its beautiful seventeenth century screen work, has a pew-end with date and initials, "W. H., 1696." *Chorley.*—A single old oak bench-end remains at the east end of the north aisle; it has the date 1671, and the initials " J. C." in a monogram. It is part of a pew pertaining to the family of Crosse of Shaw Hall. *Eccleston.*—The ancient church of St Mary retains, in the south chapel and in the nave, a number of bench-ends with carved panels from the seventeenth century seats worked up into the modern seating, with coats of arms, crests, and initials of such local families as Mawdsley, Pickering (rector), Rigbye, and Wrightington ; most of these bear the dates 1634 and 1636. A churchwardens' pew, with the wardens' names and the date 1673, is also preserved. At *Halsall* parts of the fine old stalls remain, good and deeply cut work towards the end of the fifteenth century. They were rearranged at the last restoration ; there are six old stalls on the south, and one on the north. They retain their ancient carved misericords. Some of the old desks remain, with boldly carved fronts and finials at the ends. One of the finials has the Stanley eagle and child, and another a standing lion (111). *Farnworth*, near Widnes.—The church of St Luke, almost entirely rebuilt at different periods during last century, was formerly dedicated to St Wilfrid. Here there is a seventeenth century bench with two carved ends in the vestry. Until 1894 the church was filled with seventeenth and eighteenth century pews, many of which had crests or initials of owners, with dates cut on them ; some of these inscriptions have been preserved and used as panellings to the walls. Various fifteenth and sixteenth century bench-ends then came to light, but were considered too damaged to be retained. *Great Harwood.* — Under the tower of the church of St Bartholomew is preserved an old bench with a poppy-head, and along the front is carved "*Orate p̄' aiab', Hugois Stanworth et Letecie uxor ei' qui fieri istu'. . . ."* *Hoole.*—In the church of

Sefton, Lancs.

St Michael are two seventeenth century bench-ends at the west end of the nave, bearing respectively the initials " R.O." and " F.O." *Langho.*—In the chapel of St Leonard are a number of bench-

15

ends with initials and dates of the close of the seventeenth century ; the majority are dated 1687. *Samlesbury.*—The church of St Leonard has some interesting fittings chiefly of the eighteenth century, but there are three pew-ends dated respectively 1685, 1689, and 1697. There are, however, twenty-five pews dated and initialed from 1713 to 1756. In the south aisle the old Houghton pew, with initials, arms, crest, and motto, is dated 1678. *Sefton.*—Both blocks of seats in the nave of this interesting church, twelve on each side, have good poppy-heads and well-carved bench-ends ; they date *c.* 1520-1535. Those on the north block have crowned fleur-de-lis on the four corner bench ends, and the rest have chiefly conventional floral designs. In the south block the corner seats have the Molyneaux cross, whilst the rest have the letters of the alphabet in due succession, with the exception of J, U, W, X, and Z. T, however, occurs twice, but in different designs. The emblems of the Passion occur in various places, as well as certain obscure devices. At the west end of the south aisle is a churchwardens' pew with linenfold panelling (113).[1] *Standish.*—The church of St Wilfrid retains two oak bench-ends in the north vestry, carved respectively with " E. H. 1625," and " W. R. 1626." There is also a bench under the tower, of like date, one end of which has the Worthington crest, and the other the Langtree arms and crest. *Tunstall.*—This church retains a square pew at the east end, dated 1738. *Upholland.*—In the north and south aisles of the church of St Thomas the Martyr are fifty seventeenth century bench-ends, twenty-five in each aisle, all carved with the initials of the holders, and the majority of them dated 1635. At the west end of the nave is a churchwardens' pew with the names of the wardens, and the date 1673. All the bench-ends have graded tops, somewhat after the fashion of poppy-heads. *Warton.*—In the seats of the church of St Oswald are four oak panels from old seats. One is dated 1571, with the initials " T. B." ; two have the initials of Sir Robert Bindloss of Borwick and his wife, dated 1613 ; and the fourth is dated 1612. *Woodplumpton.*—Some old pew-ends are used up as panelling along the walls ; dates 1716 to 1746.

LEICESTERSHIRE

LEICESTERSHIRE—the striking beauty and interest of so many of the churches of this county, both town and country, has not as yet been generally recognised—is rich in the remains

[1] See the good account and illustrations in Caroe and Gordon's " Sefton " (1893).

of ancient seating. In several cases its rude benches are probably the oldest in any part of England. Stall work is exceptional, though the stall-ends of Barkestone are most notable, but striking bench-ends, of which the best are at Dunton Bassett (fourteenth century), Gaddesby (thirteenth century), and Stockerstone (fifteenth century), are by no means infrequent. *Ab-Kettleby* possesses a set of sixteen benches with traceried panel ends and finials, fifteenth century. At *Aylestone*, which claims to have the largest village chancel in England, there is some old woodwork in the seating, notwithstanding the severity of a restoration in 1894. *Barkestone* has much valuable wood-work, *c.* 1500; the best of it consists of four stall-ends, two of which now form a desk and two a sedile. They are thus described by Dr Harvey in his "Little Guide" to the county: "Both pairs have tabernacle work of indescribable richness, with various small figures, and the finer pair have in addition large figures in niches, carved in high relief in a realistic manner, the one Christ bearing the lamb, the other St James robed as a Palmer; the other pair has tracery and armorial bearings." *Belgrave* has a single stall or sedile with misericord and desk. In the church of *Brentingby* two small benches are preserved which are probably of thirteenth century date. The woodwork of *Croxton Kyrial* is of special interest, as the whole of the old fifteenth century seating is extant. Out of forty-six bench-ends, with traceried panels and poppy-heads or other finials, forty-two are ancient. *Dunton Bassett* is chiefly interesting on account of the set of twelve benches of early fourteenth century date in the north aisle. *Gaddesby*, the most beautiful of Leicestershire's churches, has a number of rude plain benches of an exceptionally early date; they are coeval with the earlier portions of the present fabric, that is to say, the second quarter of the thirteenth century. *Goadby Marwood* has some old benches, probably of the fourteenth century; there are also some early benches at *Hoby*, the ends of which have poppy-heads. Two of the *Leicester* churches possess remnants of old seating; *St Martin's* has three old stalls with desks, which serve as sedilia, whilst *All Saints'* has a seventeenth century mayoral chair. *St Margaret's* used to possess old stalls, but they are now in the church of Aston juxta Birmingham. *Misterton* possesses a well-executed set of bench-ends of the seventeenth century. At *Noseley* there are double ranges of stalls, *c.* 1510, six on each side, with misericords and desks; the stall-ends bear tracery, and are crowned with large figures of cocks, the crest of the Stauntons. At *Peatling Magna* there are two benches with poppy-heads, *c.* 1400, in the chancel, and two later Perpendicular seats in the nave. *Saxilby* has some fifteenth century benches, and *Sheepshed* numerous benches with carved finials. There are also various old benches at *Stoke Golding*, *Stonesby*, and *Stretton Parva*, while *Thedding-worth* has some Perpendicular pewing. *Stockerstone*, among other interesting features, has a set of twenty-nine fifteenth century beautifully carved bench-ends. At *Thornton* we find a complete set of seats with linenfold panels, *c.* 1500. Lastly, *Wartnaby* retains two early benches.

LINCOLNSHIRE

LINCOLNSHIRE is well represented in the amount of surviving mediæval sitting. The two magnificent series of canopied stalls, both about the same date—*Lincoln Minster* and *Boston* have been discussed in a previous volume of Mr Bond's series. Brief comments are offered upon the remainder (though it makes no claim to be a complete list) in alpha-betical order. *Addlethorpe* has a wealth of old carved wood work, possibly the best of any village church in the shire ; it is seated throughout with the original fifteenth century benches, with good poppy-head finials and elbow rests. *Bratoft* has some good bench-ends in the quire, with poppy-head finials. *South Cockerington* possesses some good old bench-ends. At *Coleby* there are also good fifteenth century bench-ends, which were brought here from Hackthorn church, when the latter parish were foolish enough to eject them in favour of modern successors. The small church of *Cotes-by-Stow* has some old oak benches, four on the one side and three on the other. There is also some old benching at *Covenham St Bartholomew*. In the fine but sadly neglected church of *Croft* is a good series of fifteenth century poppy-headed and elbowed bench-ends, with traceried panels and embattled work at the fronts and backs of the end seats. There are several old oak benches at *Digby*. The seating of *Edenham* church includes some good Perpendicular seats and bench-ends. A good deal of the old seating has disappeared since 1804, when a long description in the "Gentleman's Magazine" stated that : "The pews, apparently coeval with the tower (Henry VI.), are of oak, open at the ends, perforated in the form of quatrefoils at the sides, and ornamented in the carving of pointed arches at the ends." At *Ewerby* there are some old benches with poppy-heads in the chancel. Some old bench-ends also remain at *Fenton* and *Folkingham*. Amongst other good woodwork at *Grimoldby*, there are several bench-ends. The old benches

T. B.

T. B.

T. B.

T. B.

Osbournby, Lincolnshire

of *Haconby* are noteworthy. *Halton Holgate* has a remarkable series of fine poppy-head finials to the standards throughout the church. The standards themselves are plain, but well moulded, and have elbow rests. The large majority of poppy-heads are original, but some of the taller ones of the front benches were renewed in 1845 ; these were copied from old ones in the church of *Winthorpe*. The lower part of the poppy-head is usually formed of two figures back to back, such as human grotesques or birds. A pair of owls and a pair of pelicans are cleverly carved. Another head is formed out of eight monkeys cunningly intermingled, whilst there is a single instance of a coat of arms surmounted by a towering helm and crest. All the old ones were of fifteenth century date ; they number twenty-eight. The sittings of *Haltham* have rudely carved late poppy-heads. The fine church of *Helpingham* has plain high sixteenth century benches. At *Huxley* there are a few carved seats of the fifteenth century. *Ingoldsby* possesses a good deal of fine oak seating, after the fashion of the Addlethorpe benches. The late Perpendicular carved benches of *Kelby* came from the chapel of Culverthorpe Hall. In the fine fifteenth century chancel of *Leverton* are the original stalls with poppy-head finials at the ends ; they are set on a stone wall pierced with quatrefoils. *Marshchapel* is seated throughout in old oak. *Osbournby* has a large number of interesting carved seats with singular poppy-heads remaining ; the bench-ends are very varied ; some are traceried, but others of them have small figure subjects in the upper parts, such as Adam and Eve, St George and the Dragon, and a fox preaching to geese ; they are *c.* 1500 (117). *Quarrington* has some Perpendicular bench-ends, and the like is the case with *Rauceby* and *Skendleby*. *Roughton* has some seats with late debased poppy-heads like those of Haltham. Most of the old bench-ends yet remain in the beautiful church of *Silk Willoughby*. *Scrivelsby* has lost its square-headed bench-ends ; one of them, ejected in the 'eighties of last century, when in a rotten condition, forms part of the old oak collection of Mr W. J. Andrew, F.S.A., of Michelmersh ; it has a traceried pattern of late fifteenth century date. In the parish church of *Sempringham* (no part of the old priory, as usually asserted) are some old fifteenth century benches. At *North Somercotes* six old poppy-headed elbowed bench-ends are used up in the chancel sittings. The chapel of Browne's Hospital, *Stamford*, founded in 1480, has original stalls and bench-ends. The remarkable old church of *Stow* has some graceful stall-ends in the chancel, with early fifteenth century tracery, made up in 1864 from old screen work ; in the nave are some fifteenth

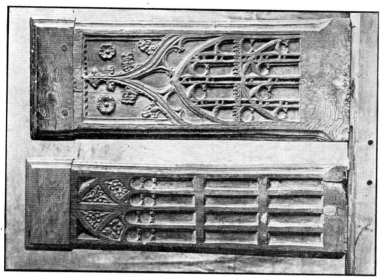

Walcot, Lincs.

H. W.

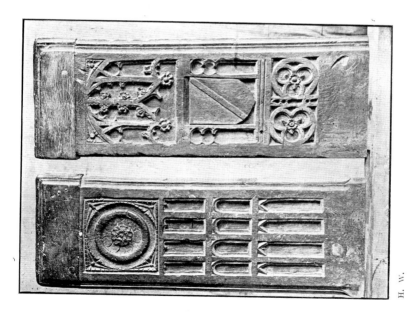

Walcot, Lincs.

H. W.

century benches, with square-headed embattled standards. At *Strubby* there are a few poppy-headed bench-ends. *Swaton* has some good fifteenth century stalls. At *Swineshead* there is much old seating with bench-ends in the south aisle. There are numerous bench-ends at *Theddlethorpe All Saints*, some of which have been made up with parts of screen tracery. There are also several good modern ones, the work of local craftsmen ; a litany desk has been constructed out of two narrow bench-ends with poppy-heads. The old collegiate church of *Tattershall* still retains some of its old stall work and tracery at the top of the panels, though the chancel windows remained unglazed for nearly half of the eighteenth century. At *North Thoresby* there are various late poppy-headed bench-ends ; on one of the standards are the initials " R.M., P.W." At *Thorpe St Peter* there is some fifteenth century seating extant, and at *Thurlby-by-Newark* there are many good bench-ends. In the nave of *Threckingham* there are some singularly late standards. *Walcot* possesses exceptionally good and clear-cut carvings on a number of square-headed bench-ends or standards of advanced fifteenth century date, as can be seen readily even from the examples here adduced (119). There is some good work in the benches of *Welby*, and *Wellington* has several good bench-ends in the north aisle. There is also some old seating in the chancel of *Westborough*. At *Wigtoft* there are two chairs formed from bench-ends ; while at *Wilsford* several old bench-ends are still standing. *Winthorpe* is thought by some to carry the palm of all the Lincolnshire mediæval seating. The body of the church is fitted throughout with old late fifteenth century benching, with poppy-heads and carved elbows. In the chancel are four singularly beautiful and elaborately carved stall-ends, of considerable size, having a height, exclusive of the platform, of 58½ inches. The best of these is on the south side of the re-turned stalls ; it is a mass of beautiful tracery and foliage, and exhibits in the centre of the panel the legend of St Hubert found in the forest by a stag that bore a rood or crucifix between its horns. The poppy-head of this stall-end is thick with exquisitely carved acorns and oak leaves, and up, as it were, the branches of this tree climb three little manikins, one of whom has caught a bird. *Yarborough* is the last Lincolnshire church to be here chronicled as retaining some old bench-ends.

MIDDLESEX

Open oak seats of pre-Reformation dates used to prevail in many of the Middlesex churches, having buttressed standard ends, but so-called restoration has swept most of them away. The earliest register book of *Hadley*, beginning in 1619, records the numerous benefactions of Thomas Emerson, lord of the manor. In 1609 he beautified the whole of the interior, re-pewing it in wainscot, but this disappeared under Mr Street in 1848-56, when infinite pains were taken to make the fabric as new as possible both inside and out. A clean sweep was made of all the old fittings of *Hanworth* church, including delightful benches and bench-ends of fifteenth century date, in 1865, under a scheme of restoration and preposterous expansion utterly out of keeping with the surroundings of this country church. *Harefield* church was so completely "refitted, enlarged, and beautified" by the late Mr Newdegate in 1840, that there is nothing left of any interest except numerous costly family monuments. Some rich oak carving of late Renaissance date, the spoils of a Belgian religious house, are worked up into stalls and a reredos in the chancel. The disastrous restoration fever raged fiercely throughout this small county during last century among all the finer churches, such as *Harrow* (1847), *Hayes* (1873), *Hillingdon* (1868), *Pinner* (1879), *Ruislip* (1869), and *West Drayton* (1898); their previous condition can be gleaned from an admirable and now rare little volume by Rev. J. H. Sperling, entitled "Church Walks in Middlesex"; it was first published in 1849, and a second enlarged edition in 1853. Mr Sperling wrote of *Harlington* that "the western half of the nave retains its old open seats with buttressed standards, in excellent preservation." This church was, however, "completely restored in 1880," and these village mediæval seats were of course not smart enough for Victorian taste. There is, however, much good pre-Reformation seating still left at *Harmondsworth*, with buttressed standards; the date is of the first quarter of the sixteenth century. *Littleton* is another exception; the seats in the nave are *c.* 1500. Among some old oak panelling, taken from former pewing in *Northolt* church, appears the following inscription: "William Rouse and Mathew Hunt, Church-wardens, 1629." At *Ruislip* four of the old oak benches of the usual Middlesex type have been suffered to remain at the west end, but scores of a like pattern fell victims to Scott's destructive restoration of 1869. Most of the present seating of the nave of *Stepney* is made up of oak panelling of eighteenth century date, which previously pertained to the old high pews ; in a west gallery is a single fine fifteenth century example of a poppy-headed bench-end.

MONMOUTH

There is a strange absence of any trace of mediæval seatings among the churches of the little county of Monmouth. In fact, though we know the county fairly well, we have no knowledge of anything of the kind save at *Abergavenny*. The church of St Mary in that town, originally the church of an alien Benedictine priory, retains in the quire twenty-four canopied misericord stalls, one of which bears on a bench-end " Wynchester," the name of a former prior. Of early seventeenth century work there is a good example of a well-carved box canopied pew in the church of *Skenfrith* ; it belonged to the family of Maughan.

NORFOLK

Out of six hundred and fifty old churches of NORFOLK still extant, upwards of one hundred and ten retain traces of pre-Reformation seating, chiefly of fifteenth or early sixteenth century date, but with here and there carving of an indubitable fourteenth century type.

As to quire stalls, they are to be noted at Aylsham (1507), Binham, Blakeney, Castleacre (three misericords), Castor (two misericords), Cawston (1460), Cley and East Harling (six misericords each), Horning, Ingham, Litcham, Lynn St Margaret (sixteen misericords), Lynn St Nicholas (ten misericords, now in the Museum of the Architectural Association, London), Norwich, St Andrew, St Michael Coslany, St Gregory, St Peter Mancroft and St Swithun, Sall, Sprowston, Thompson (four misericords), Tilney All Saints (eighteen misericords), Trunch, Walpole St Peter (five misericords), North Walsham, Old Walsingham, Walsoken (nine misericords), and Wiggenhall St Mary Magdalene. Many of the stalls have poppy-headed ends.

This county, not excepting Suffolk, stands pre-eminent for the number and occasional beauty of the pre-Reformation benches and bench-ends (usually with poppy-heads) which are still surviving. They are found in the greatest number in north-east Norfolk, throughout the Broads district, where easy water-carriage facilitated the bringing of timber from distant parts. The nave and aisle of the little church of *Irstead* have the old sittings throughout, and the same may be said of the much larger churches of *Wiggenhall St Mary* and *South Walsham St Mary.* It is also nearly the case with the much smaller church of *Horsey.*

The simplest form of the old benching consists of substantial slabs of oak, with poppy-head bench-ends, but no backs. Good instances of this may be noted at *Cawston* and *East Winch,* where they are still in use (125). A few solitary cases of the survival of a backless bench are to be seen up and down

C. F. N.

Wiggenhall St German, Norfolk

the county, where they are stowed away as lumber under the tower, or placed in the porch. In the nave of *Palling* church are fourteen old benches of the end of the fifteenth century, with fairly good poppy-heads, but they are much spoilt by the liberal use of modern paint, and by being supplied with backs of poor deal. Within the recollection of the writer, whole rows of backless benches have been swept away out of five churches.

Omitting for lack of space about twenty churches, of which we have notes as to the old sitting, a few details are now set forth of the more valuable remains. In the very small church of *Ashmanhaugh* there are twelve old poppy-headed bench-ends, also a piece of seat panelling in which each of the Wounds is severally carved, together with a like number of shields bearing initial letters. *Aylemeston* has a fine piece of late eleventh century stalling. *Barton Turf* has six old poppy-head ends affixed to the quire seats. Several of the old seats of *Beeston-next-Mileham* have carved backs and poppy-head ends. Twelve of the old Perpendicular benches of *Binham* have poppy-head ends and good tracery in the backs. *Blakeney* has chancel

C. F. N.

Great Walsingham, Norfolk

stalls of two designs ; four of these on the north side stood in the nave before the restoration. There are also some really good poppy-heads at *Brinton, Brisley*, and *Great Carbrooke*. At *Cley* there are several very good standard ends of fifteenth century date, worked up into pews seventy years ago ; there are also six stalls with misericords in the chancel. (See *Norf. Arch.*, vol. xiv.) There are some admirable examples of fifteenth century seatings in the naves of *South Creyke, South Elmham*, and *Field Dalling*. Both the aisles of *Garboldisham* are seated throughout with good fifteenth century benches. In the chancel of *Horning* are four cunningly carved late bench-ends ; one has a realistic demon thrusting a man into a dragon's jaw, doubtless intended to represent Hell; on another is a man strangling a serpent, representing Sin; a third has a crosier; whilst the fourth is richly floriated. There are also various good poppy-heads in the body of the church. Under the central tower of *South Lopham* there are some remains of old poppy-headed seats. On one of the poppy-heads is carved an elephant and castle, the badge of the Beaumont family; Katherine, Duchess of Norfolk, held the manor of Lopham in

C. F. N.

Cawston, Norfolk

dower after the duke's death in 1432, and she married for her second husband John Vivien Beaumont, who was killed in battle, 1460. The date of this poppy-head is consequently 1450-60 (see *Norf. Arch.*, vols. xii. and xiv.). At *Ludham* there are various old poppy-headed bench-ends worked up in the seating. There used to be a grand series of poppy-heads in both chancel and nave of *St Nicholas Lynn*, but most of them have found their way to the Architectural Museum in Tufton Street, Westminster. At *Narborough* there are several fifteenth century benches, their ends carved with a variety of local armorial bearings. At *Pulham St Mary* there is an exceptionally fine set of fifteenth century seats and benches, both in the nave and aisle. The poppy-heads of *Runton* are quaint and well

Wiggenhall St Mary, Norfolk

Wiggenhall St Mary, Norfolk

executed; and those of *Salthouse* are also exceptionally good. At *Saxthorpe* two old poppy-head bench-ends bear the letter " P "; Peter Page was vicar here from 1482-1536. At the west end of the nave of *Shouldham* are several old seats, some with poppy-heads, and others with square-headed bench-ends carved in tracery like those of the West of England. The poppy-headed bench-ends of *Sheringham* are well worth studying ; several of them have quaint animals carved on the elbows, including a mermaid, and a baby in swaddling clothes (129). In the south aisle of *Southacre* is a fine set of embattled seats, with poppy-head ends of late fifteenth century date. At *Sparham* there are some good original benches with traceried backs. The Pedlar's Seat, *Swaffham*, displays the carved fifteenth century figures of John Chapman (the builder of the north aisle) and his wife, Catherine, together with a pedlar and his dog, worked up into a prayer desk ; Sir L. Gomme has dealt at length with this Swaffham legend, giving three illustrations of the woodwork in his recent book, " Folklore as an Historic Science." In the quire of *Thompson* are eleven old stalls bearing the Shardlow arms, a chevron between three cross crosslets fitchée. Only four of them retain the misericords ; there are also a number of old oak benches with poppy-heads of various designs. There are six massive oak benches in the nave of *Thornham*, with fine poppy-heads, and quaint coarse carvings at the elbows ; one of these has a chalice and wafer twice repeated, and another a windmill. *Tuttington* has many curiously carved bench-ends. *North Walsham* has one or two noteworthy large poppy-heads in connection with the stalls. *South Walsham St Mary* is second to Wiggenhall St Mary in the completeness of its old seating of late fifteenth century date ; several of the poppy-heads bear in their centre single letters, such as " T " and " R," denoting the owners or donors of the seats ; others have brief inscriptions in small black-letter text. *Old Walsingham* has a very fine series of fifteenth century seats with fretted backs ; the ends have well-developed poppy-head finials, and quaint figures on some of the shoulders (13). The old seats of *Wiggenhall St Mary* are the best in the kingdom, and are almost perfect in their original fifteenth century condition. There is profuse variation in the details of the carving ; the ends all terminate in fine poppy-heads, with small seated figures on each side, whilst a larger figure of a saint on a pedestal under a canopy occupies the face of the bench-ends in the central alley ; the backs of the seats are pierced with quatrefoils or flowing tracery (128). *Wiggenhall St German* has also a rich supply of poppy-headed bench-ends, and the backs of the benches themselves are beautifully carved with pierced quatrefoils ; but a good deal of the work is new or successfully restored. The particular feature of the standards are the grotesques projecting on each side below the poppy-heads

(123).   *Walsoken* has some fine elaborate bench-ends, resembling those of the two Wiggenhalls, and rivals the last-named

Walsoken, Norfolk

F. B.

Wiggenhall St Mary, Norfolk

C. F. N.

church in the beauty of the ends and backs of its benches, though not in their completeness ; the carvings on the shoulders

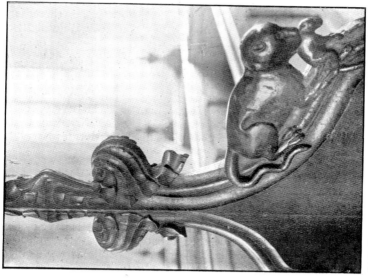

Sheringham, Norfolk

Sheringham, Norfolk

of some are exceptionally quaint (128). At *East Winch*, in addition to the backless row in the north aisle, there is a delightful row of small fifteenth century benches with embattled backs and poppy-head finials.

As to post-Reformation old seatings, the following are worthy of mention in chronological order. At *Bressingham* the seating is of the year 1527, at which date the whole church was rebuilt. Some poor attempts at outline poppy-headed bench-ends are believed to be of the year 1587, which date is rudely carved on the reading-desk. In the chancel of *Beeston St Mary* hangs a board on which is painted the following black-letter inscription with rubricated initials :—

"Johnes Forbye artiû magister atqu' huius Ecclie Rector hasce Tabulas, hec sacraria istaqu' subsellia refecit, et sacris posuit nō proptfan:s aut scholarib' usibus. Mors mihi vita."

It will scarcely be credited that modern Vandals have ejected the oak stalls, supplied by pious Master Forby three centuries ago, to make way for successors of sticky pine. Part of the ornamental panelling of the quire stalls of *Irstead* is dated 1663. At *Swanton Morley* there are a set of plain and roughly cut solid benches and ends which we believe to be of Laudian date.

NORTHAMPTON

The county of NORTHAMPTON, so justly renowned for its churches, is well off in the remains of mediæval sittings ; both in numbers and in execution. *Great Addington* has some plain benches, *c.* 1500. There is a certain amount of seating at *Ashby St Ledgers* coeval with the beautiful fifteenth century rood-screen. Some rude benches at *Little Billing* were considered by Parker (1849) to be fourteenth century, but they are all gone ; their successors are new ones of deal, painted brown. *Benefield* has three of the misericord stalls which were dispersed from the collegiate church of Foth ringhay. The fifteenth century quire stalls of *Blisworth* have good poppy-heads. *Bozeat* retains the whole of its fifteenth century benches ; very plain and simple. *Brington* is seated throughout with massive oak benches, the standards of which carry armorial shields and terminate in poppy-headed finials. It is usually supposed, and has been several times stated, that these seats are all of the fifteenth century ; but this is far from being the case. The majority of them only date from 1847, when Earl Spencer

Higham Ferrers, Northants

removed various high pews and had the then extant heraldic benches closely imitated. The armorial bearings on the old examples prove that they were executed between 1445 and 1457. The arms of Grey and Ferrers are repeated several times, together with those of Lord Grey's mother, who was an heiress of Astley. The panels of the seat-ends of *Byfield, c.* 1450, are excellent examples of Northants carpentry ; the square-headed standards have shallow buttresses, and good tracery at the top of the panels. *Clay Coton* and *Cold Ashby* have some such remnants of pre-Reformation seating, but of no particular importance. At *Catesby* there are some seats or benches, *temp.* Charles I. There are some old benches in the nave of *Creaton.* When Mr Micklethwaite reported on the church of *Croughton* in 1872, he considered the date of the old pewing to be *c.* 1490. There are four blocks of these old seats to the east and west of the cross passage between the doors. The square-headed standards have good traceried heads, with some unusual designs at the base ; on one is carved a chalice and wafer. The open seating of *Cranford St Andrew* is often supposed to be mediæval, but it only dates from 1847, when various panels of foreign Renaissance carving were introduced. The chancel of *Dodding-ton* retains four fifteenth century stalls. *Draughton,* though drastically restored, has some finely panelled fifteenth century bench-ends. *Duston* has a few old mediæval seats. *Easton-on-the-Hill* has seven rows of solid benches, dated 1631. *Fawsley* has a considerable amount of grotesque carving of Perpendicular date from the old bench-ends reused in the later seating. *Finedon* is justly celebrated for its fine pewing throughout the church in the latter part of the fifteenth century ; the square-headed standards are beautifully wrought in tracery both at the top and base of the panels, and buttressed. Parker (1849) considered them the earliest known instance of doors to early seating, but the doors were all removed some years ago. In the chancel of *Gayton* there are six good stalls, *c.* 1500. Parker (1849) says of *Hargrave* : " The benches in the nave are of very fair design ; some benches have the linen pattern, and one has a carved finial ; their date may be of the reign of Henry VI." It seems, however, that the seating of this church was carried out towards the beginning of the sixteenth century. T. Bocker, in his will of 1525, says : " I bequeth to the setyng of the church xxd." *Hazelbeach* was much restored in 1860, but the six old oak seats of fifteenth century date, well carved, were carefully preserved, and new ones supplied after the like pattern. *Hemington,* which was much restored in 1872, has in the new chancel two of the beautiful somewhat restored

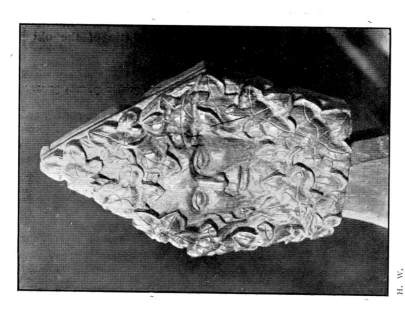

Ufford, Northants

H. W.

Ufford, Northants

H. W.

stalls which used to be in the collegiate church of Fotheringhay. This fifteenth century work is of great merit, both in the standards and the misericords; the former are of exceptional design, the upper ends curling round somewhat after the fashion of a pastoral staff. *Higham Ferrers* has ten very fine canopied stalls on each side of the quire, *c.* 1415 ; the first on the south side has the carved head of Archbishop Chichele, and the first on the north side bears the impaled arms of Chichele and the See of Canterbury. The arms of the stalls have well-carved elbow pieces (131). In the new chancel of *Holdenby* there are six misericord stalls of early fifteenth century date. *Irchester* has a few old fifteenth century seats, with the standards carved with beautiful tracery and buttressed. The eight old misericord stalls of *Irthlingborough* date from 1485 ; they have small poppy-heads ; the desks are plain. In the nave there are considerable remains of the old benches. *Isham* was thoroughly restored and reseated in 1870, but there are two old stalls in the chancel. Some old bench-ends at *Kingscliffe*, together with traceried panels in pulpit and reading-desk, came from Fotheringhay church. Much of the church of *Kingsthorpe* was rebuilt and the interior gutted in 1863, but a little of the old fifteenth century woodwork was spared. Illustrations are given of three vigorous but rather coarsely executed poppy-heads in the Rev. R. M. Serjeantson's " History of the Church of St Peter, Northampton," the mother church of Kingsthorpe. *Lowick* was restored and reseated in 1864, but a little of the old sittings remains ; a poppy-head to a fifteenth century bench-end shows a pair of well-carved human heads. *Luddington-in-the-Brook* retains numerous old seats of a curious pattern. At *Maxey* there are some old poppy-headed bench-ends. *Middleton Cheney* has some good woodwork ; the chancel stalls have been much restored, but the finials of archangels with out-spread wings at the east end on the standards are unusual and noteworthy. At *Newton Bromshold* there are a few mediæval benches. The chancel of *Passenham* has seven stalls richly carved on each side in niches supported by Ionic pillars ; each niche bears the name of an apostle or saint in gilt letters. They were placed here in 1638. *Peterborough* cathedral has three old stalls, *c.* 1450. Parker (1849) says of *Raunds* that several of the old benches remained, but they had been heightened with deal and turned into modern pews. All this was, however, changed under a great restoration by Scott in 1870, and a fair amount of old work remains. *Ravensthorpe* retains some good benches of late fifteenth century date ; the standards are square-headed with good tracery. *Ringstead* and *Rushden* have each some remains of early seating. At *Rothwell* there are seven late fifteenth century stalls. The adjacent churches of *Slipton* and *Twywell* also retain some old benches. *Spratton* was severely restored and reseated in 1847, but several of the seats retain pre-Reformation work. *Stanwick*, restored in 1856, also retains some old plain benches. At *Tansor* there are six misericord stalls from Fotheringhay, also some fifteenth century benches with poppy-headed standards. *Ufford* was reseated in 1860, but it retains some highly remarkable poppy-heads, with quaint human faces enveloped in foliage, of which two examples are given in the plates (133). *Warkworth* has good early bench-ends worked up into modern pews. One has a carving of two men and a woman kneeling before an altar, with an open book inscribed "Sancta Maria, Ora pro nobis." Another is a representation of the Annunciation ; it shows the archangel with a large lily pot. The open seats of *Warmington* with poppy-headed finials have taken-in more than one ecclesiologist, who has considered them early pre-Reformation, but they merely date from an extensive restoration of 1879. *Wellingborough* has seven stalls, *c.* 1385. At *Winwick* there is a single stall, *c.* 1500. *Whiston* has some original seats of the year 1534. The church of *Woodford*, near Byfield, was very extensively restored in 1878, but the fifteenth century oak bench-work was incorporated with the new seating. At *Velvertoft* the old pews were removed in 1870, but some very fine fifteenth century benches were found. It may be added that at *Denford* there are seven stone stalls, and at *Kings Sutton* twelve resembling sedilia.

NORTHUMBERLAND

NORTHUMBERLAND is almost entirely destitute of ancient seating. The reason for the absence is not far to seek. So large a portion of the country being immediately contiguous to Scotland, the whole area was peculiarly subject to border raids ; and this not only during the centuries when the two kingdoms were definitely at war, but even as late as Elizabeth's reign, when the less scrupulous of the Scots came across the border for the avowed purpose of looting the cattle and setting fire to the churches, to which the inhabitants resorted for refuge. We have a fair personal knowledge of the county, and have no recollection of having seen a single scrap of mediæval sitting, save at the abbey church of *Hexham*. Nor do we find a single reference to old seating in the ten fine volumes of the "County History" already published. The fifteenth century ritual arrangements of the grand abbey church of *Hexham* remained perfect up to 1858, though somewhat obscured by pews and galleries, but in that year a shameless clearance of the whole was made under the specious name of restoration—thirty-eight stalls and four most exceptional timber sedilia. Fortunately a good deal of the rejected woodwork did not leave Hexham, and in 1888 most of the stall work and sedilia were recovered and reinstated in a restored condition. The poppy-headed stall work of St Michael's, *Alnwick*, is sometimes pointed out as mediæval, but it is merely good local work of 1875.

NOTTINGHAMSHIRE

NOTTINGHAMSHIRE, as has been already remarked, possesses in its churches an unusual number of stone bench-tables. As it is of comparatively small area, it compares favourably with most counties in the survival of old sittings both in chancel and nave. As to stalls with misericords, they have been fully treated in another volume in this series, but it may be concisely recapitulated that there are at Newark twenty-five; at Sneinton eight; at Wysall four; at Thurgarton three; at Strelley two; and at Somerton one. At North Collingham a row of misericords, divorced from their stalls, have been most foolishly stuck up over the chancel arch. Benches and bench-ends are fairly frequent. The best are at Balderton, Barnby-in-the-Willows, and Holme. It will be well now to discuss them briefly in order.[1] *Attenborough.*—On the north side of the chancel are two finely carved poppy-headed stall-ends, *c.* 1500, standing 6 ft. 6 in. high. Also several panels of fine Jacobean Renaissance work, arranged horizontally, of mermen and mermaids with elaborately convoluted tails. They bear the initials "J. P.," and a shield of arms, a fesse between three cinquefoils. These are the arms of John Powtrell, son of Walter Powtrell, of West Hallam, Derbyshire, by his wife Cassandra, daughter of Francis Strelley. The Strelley arms, paly of six, also appear in this carving. Against the north wall is a wooden shield bearing the quartered arms of Powtrell. *Balderton.*—In this church there are no fewer than forty-five benches of the end of the fifteenth century, with good, slightly

[1] See "Nottinghamshire Churches," by Rev. Dr Cox, in County Church Series.

varied tracery on the standard ends in three tiers, but mostly of a stiff character (11). A large majority of the poppy-heads are ornamented with a realistic couple of rabbits, heads downwards (illustrations of these bench-ends appeared in the "Builder" of 1845, p. 331). *Barnby-in-the-Willows.*—In the nave are twenty odd benches, with well-carved traceried ends and poppy-heads of fifteenth century design ; a few have been reproduced in cast iron ! In the chancel are quire benches of the same kind with panelled tracery in front. *Car Colston.*—At the west end are four old fifteenth century bench-ends hacked down. *Costock.*— There are here six old fifteenth century poppy-headed bench-ends. The late rector (Rev. C. G. Millard) was successful in producing sixty-five modern imitations. *Cropwell Bishop.*—At the west end are five really good old benches with poppy-head ends of late fourteenth century or early fifteenth century date. *Edwalton.*—In the north adjunct to the chancel are two old benches ; the ends show that they are fourteenth century, but repaired towards the close of the fifteenth century. *Gedling.*—The pulpit, which was made up in 1886, is partly constructed out of the remains of bench-ends. *Granby.*—There are fourteen old benches in the nave with good poppy-head ends ; on one is a mermaid. *Hawton* has a considerable number of plain massive oak benches carved with the Perpendicular tower, which was erected by Sir Thomas Molineux, *ob.* 1491. *Hickling* has a few good bench-ends, *c.* 1400. *Hockerton.*—There is a bench-end under the church tower dated 1599. *Holme.*—The south chancel chapel is fitted throughout with good massive benches and stalls of the end of the fifteenth century (11); the ends are finely carved with angels, birds, animals, and grotesques (see "Thoroton Society Proceedings," vol. iv., and more especially Mr Ewart Woolley's recent pamphlet on the church). *Kneesall.*—There are some good fifteenth century benches. *East Leake.*—There are a few poppy-head bench-ends of the fifteenth century, including a well-designed pelican in her piety. *West Leake.*—Two substantial oak benches with roll-moulding are the only remains of pre-Reformation seating. *Maplebeck* has some seventeenth century panelled oak benches. *Newark.*—In addition to the fine series of stalls (twenty-five), there are some late fifteenth century bench-ends ; there are drawings of them in the "Architectural Association Sketch Book," 1st Series, vol. viii. *Normanton-on-Soar.*—In both the transepts are some plain heavy oak seats of late fifteenth century or early sixteenth century date. *Sibthorpe.*—At the west end of this most interesting church are a few plain solid oak pre-Reformation benches. *Sneinton.*—The good series of stalls with misericords were purchased from

18

St Mary's, Nottingham, in 1848. *Sutton-cum-Lound.*—There is some vine-trail moulding on the backs of two chancel benches, taken from the old rood-screen. On the south side of the nave are nine old benches with traceried ends and poppy-heads. *Sutton-on-Trent.*—There are some old stall-ends in the chancel. *Walesby.*—Here there are eight stout benches of early sixteenth century date. *Walkeringham* has a few old benches with squared ends. *North Wheatley* has several old benches with traceried ends, *c.* 1510. One or two of these were rescued from the destroyed churches of *South Wheatley* and *West Burton.* *Wysall* has a few pre-Reformation benches at the west end.

OXFORDSHIRE

The county of OXFORD, justly celebrated for the interest and beauty of so large a proportion of its churches, is distinctly limited in the number that retain even traces of their ancient sittings. Doubtless this partly arises from the fierceness with which the restoration fever raged within its limits during the third quarter of last century. In the quire of *Brampton* there are certain fifteenth century well-carved stalls, with misericords and poppy-headed bench-ends. At *Bicester* a few of the Perpendicular benches remain. The small church of *Chastleton* has a few carved bench-ends. There are some good square-headed bench-ends at *Hampton Poyle* ; ten of them are given in the " Architectural Association Sketch Book," 1st Series, vol. iii. At *Hornton* a portion of the old screen is used as the back of a chancel pew. The ten stalls of *Kidlington* have their desks formed of good thirteenth century square-headed bench-ends, moved here from the nave. These ends are supported by shallow buttresses on each side, whilst the central panels are well and boldly carved with tracery and other devices, as shown in the plates ; the one of a pelican vulning itself is specially effective. Two good poppy-heads are illustrated from the interesting village church of *Merton* (139). At *Milcombe* some oak benches bear Perpendicular tracery. There are a few good fifteenth century benches at *Noke.* *Oxford* has been bereft of almost all the mediæval stall work which once adorned the college chapels. The fine late Gothic stall work of *Christ Church* was removed to the so-called Latin chapel in the north-east part of the church in 1630, where it still remains with fourteen poppy-heads. The " richly wainscoated " oak substitutes were in their turn ejected in 1876 for good modern Gothic, the seventeenth century stall work being transferred

Merton, Oxon.

J. F. E.

Merton, Oxon

J. F. E.

to the church of *Cassington*, Oxfordshire. The once fine ancient stall work of *Magdalen College* chapel was shamelessly sold by auction in 1837. The original poppy-headed stall work of *Corpus Christi* chapel was removed in favour of its much inferior successor in 1676, which still remains. The grand stall work of *Merton College* chapel, erected in 1394, and decorated with figures of prophets and saints in 1493, was thrown out to make way for comparatively poor fittings in 1671. A fragment which was preserved is figured in A. Pugin's "Examples of Gothic Architecture," vol. i., p. 16 (1829). The ruined mansion, park and chapel of *Rycote*, in the parish of Great Haseley, abound in interesting associations, for here the Princess Elizabeth was entertained partly as a prisoner, and partly as a guest, during Queen Mary's reign. Charles I. was also a guest at Rycote both in 1625 and in 1643-44. The grand mansion, built here by Lord Williams in 1539, has almost disappeared, but the chapel founded here in 1449 by Richard Quartermayne, and Sybil his wife, is still standing, but in a sorry plight when we last saw it (1894). Its woodwork is of very great interest, for it extends from the year of its foundation, down to a Georgian reredos. Reference has been made above to the two remarkable state pews, but here it may be remarked that the open benching on the north side of the quasi-nave, and the larger pewing on the south side, are mainly coeval with the foundation of the chapel ; the ends and panels are supported by a series of shallow buttresses (38). The nave of *Souldern* church retains some old carved benches of fifteenth century date. In the nave of *Stanton St John* are benches of the same date ; the ends have a diversity of well-carved poppy-heads ; many of them consist of a pair of human heads. There are also many benches with carved ends in the church of *Steeple Aston*. The oak stalls, with misericords, on the south side of the quire of *Swinbrook* came from the neighbouring church of Burford. The quire stalls of *Thame* came from Thame abbey at the dissolution. There are some noteworthy carved pews at *Great Tew*, of early sixteenth century date. The chapel of the beautiful manor house of *Water Eaton*, c. 1610, on the banks of the Cherwell, shows good Jacobean carving on the pews, as well as on the pulpit and screen. Of *Yarnton* church Mr Brabant says : "The woodwork is very good throughout, comprising an old pulpit and reading desk, several pews with poppy-heads, and two excellent screens."[1]

[1] "Little Guide to Oxfordshire," p. 274.

RUTLAND

Of little RUTLAND it may be fairly said that "no area of a greater size can present a more consistently interesting series of village churches." Nevertheless, although we have visited all of them, some of them many years ago, we have not any recollection of the survival of a single remnant of early seating in any form. It may indeed be assumed that this is the case, for that careful ecclesiologist and antiquary, Mr V. B. Crowther-Beynon, does not mention a solitary case in his recent "Little Guide" to the county. On looking through Blore's "Antiquities of Rutland," published in 1811, we found a single reference to old work, namely, in the account of *Ketton* church, p. 103. He says : "Three of the ancient stalls, curiously decorated, and some of the ancient pews in a mutilated state, are still preserved." The three stalls appear on Plate XII. ; they are of ordinary fifteenth century type, and two of them show misericords.

The body of the church of *Teigh*, though dating so late as 1780, is so exceptional in its arrangement that we may be forgiven citing Mr Crowther-Beynon's account : "The seats for the congregation are arranged in ascending tiers, facing north and south like those of a college chapel. The west end of the nave is closed by a kind of screen, the upper part being painted to represent windows in the trees, etc., beyond. Below are three boxes serving for the pulpit (centre), and desks for the parson and clerk, these being approached by a staircase behind the screen."

SHROPSHIRE

SHROPSHIRE has not retained any great amount of pre-Reformation seating; it only occurs in about ten or twelve cases all told. The fine series of misericord stalls at *Ludlow* and *Tong* have already had justice done them by Mr Bond in a previous volume of this English Church Art Series. As, however, there is such a striking absence of the poppy-head ornaments elsewhere in the county, it will be well to draw attention to the remarkable and highly developed carving in these two places. One of these at *Ludlow* is well carved with a Pieta, or the Blessed Virgin with the dead Christ on her knees. Two of the most remarkable subjects treated of in the Tong poppy-heads are the Resurrection and the Ascension.

The remainder of the old wood seatings are very briefly treated in alphabetical order.

South Brent, Somerset

South Brent, Somerset

Great Bolas has some massive benches in the gallery which are *c.* 1500. The re-turned stalls of the quire of *Chirbury*, which pertained to the canons of the small Austin priory, were translated some little time ago to the church of Montgomery. At *Clee St Margaret* there are a number of very thick oak benches, *c.* 1400. In the modern north aisle of *Donnington* there are some fifteenth century seats. At *Holdgate* there are two bold standards to a seat on the north side of the chancel, which may be of late fourteenth century date ; here, too, there is a single misericord. *Ludlow*, in addition to its splendid stalls, has some Perpendicular seatings in St John's chapel. *Munslow* has ten fine old seats with square-ended standards of late fifteenth century date ; other benches and old pews were ejected at the restoration. *Stokesay*, famed for its 1654 pew, has at the west end some old fifteenth century benching. At *Tong* there are a few remnants of Perpendicular seating in addition to the stalls. A good deal of old fourteenth century benching was swept out of *Worfield* church during a drastic restoration in 1861-62, of which there are but few remnants; there is, or used to be, one of these old benches in the belfry. The massive benches in the midst of *Worthen* church are doubtless of mediæval origin, but, adds Dr Cranage, "they seem to have been partially reconstructed in that of the seating, portions of a mediæval rood-loft being largely used. The turned heads of the bench-ends are quite of Jacobean character, and in some cases are of one piece with them."

As to post-Reformation seating during the period between 1555 and 1700, Shropshire is well supplied. There is not space to attempt complete enumeration. The best examples are the fine set of pews at *North Lydbury*, *c.* 1600. Other good later instances occur at *Easthope*, 1623 ; *Edgton*, 1631 ; and *Benthall*, 1667.

SOMERSETSHIRE

SOMERSETSHIRE is justly celebrated for the multitude of its surviving bench-ends, often of great beauty. They are so numerous—a recent writer has called them legion—that it is obviously impossible in a work such as this to do more than call attention to and illustrate the more noteworthy. As a rule these Somerset bench-ends belong to the last half of the fifteenth century, down to the end of the reign of Henry VIII. They chiefly occur in the Quantock and West Somerset districts, where wood was abundant and local stone intractable. It has often been coolly assumed and sometimes almost positively

asserted that "a band of Flemish carvers" went through
Somerset and North Devon carving pew-ends about 1530-40,

Broomfield, Somerset

G. J. G.

Broomfield, Somerset

G. J. G.

introducing Renaissance designs amongst Gothic tracery. There
is not, however, so far as we are aware, a shadow of substantial

Broomfield, Somerset

G. J. G.

Broomfield, Somerset

G. J. G.

ground on which to base such an hypothesis.   Contrariwise,
there is much evidence amongst Churchwardens' Accounts and

Crowcombe Somerset

G. J. G.

Crowcombe, Somerset

G. J. G.

elsewhere to prove that this delightful craftsmanship was an
indigenous growth, the result of local effort and skill, though
based, perchance, in its later development on patterns brought

Clapton-in-Gordano, Somerset

from over the seas. These west country bench-ends are chiefly square-headed, and poppy-head finials are comparatively rare ; they are made of well-seasoned oak, thick and strong like the benches they support. Well over a thousand of these standards exist to-day in Somerset, and they are for the most part in thoroughly good preservation. The standards or bench-ends of *Banwell* are notable and varied, *c.* 1500 ; it is one of the very few churches of this county where there are poppy-head finials. They may also be noted in the neighbouring churches of *Churchill*, *Yatton*, and also at *Lovington*, *Exford*, and *Bicknoller*. At *Barton St David's* some of the old seat panels have been preserved and reused at the west end. The nave of *Balston-borough* retains a number of old fifteenth century benches ; to one of them is attached a hinged flap seat for a maid. *Barwick* has some fine bench-ends, *c.* 1533. On the door of the reading-desk are the initials " W. H.," said to be those of William Hope, at this time patron of the living. There is a fine set of bench-ends at *Bishop's Hull* ; the most singular carving is one depicting the Resurrection. Our Lord rises from the tomb amidst the three sleeping soldiers, whilst in the lower part of the same panel is the incongruous symbol of the pelican in its piety ; another striking end, near the font, presents the figure of a night watchman. In the large church of *Bishop's Lydeard*, the bench-ends of late fifteenth century date display a great variety of spirited carvings of figures, animals, foliage, and geometrical patterns, but having in all cases a double row of stiff tracery at the base. Perhaps the most striking are : (1) a three-masted ship ; (2) a windmill and birds, with the miller below ; and (3) a fleur-de-lis on a shield, with a large crown above, the latter supported by two lions rampant. Just occasionally old bench-ends show traces of original colouring, particularly in the case of heraldry ; but the profusion of red and blue paint, coarsely applied, at Bishop's Lydeard, is a comparatively modern adornment. The fifteenth century bench-ends of *East Brent* form a good and interesting set ; note the symbols of the Evangelist, though that of St Mark is missing here and also at South Brent, a charming one of the pelican in its piety, the arms of Glastonbury abbey, and the initials of John Selwood, abbot of Glastonbury, who died in 1473. *South Brent* has another excellent set, chiefly sacred emblems, *e.g.*, St Luke (142), but including the humorous mediæval legend of Reynard the Fox in three tableaux (153). At *Broomfield* there are some singularly good ends of both conventional and natural foliage ; one of them, whereon a bird is introduced on the stem of a fruitful vine, is a most effective piece of graceful design ; another

Crowcombe, Somerset

F. H. C.

Kingston, Somerset

G. J. G.

beautiful example has the duplicated IHC. monogram, though treated differently, encircled in vine trails. A third bears the

Broomfield, Somerset

G. I. G.

Crowcombe, Somerset

F. H. C.

name of Simon Werman in large capitals ; his name also appears on the *Trull* benches ; doubtless he was a craftsman of some celebrity. The continuous panels of several fronts or backs of sets of seats are also delightful. The date in this case is certainly early sixteenth century (144). The bench-ends of *North Cadbury*

Milverton, Somerset

G. J. G.

Milverton, Somerset

G. J. G.

are noteworthy and mostly curious, dating from 1538. There is a singular stiff treatment of the Five Wounds, the heart in the centre within a wreath, another has a windmill, whilst a

F. H. C.   Monksilver, Somerset

F. H. C.   Monksilver, Somerset

Trull, Somerset

W. P. W.

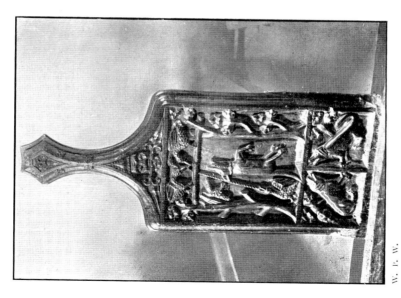

South Brent, Somerset

W. P. W.

third shows the profiled busts of a man and woman on the verge
of kissing. The front of the west gallery of *Churchstanton* is
made up of a series of good bench-ends. On one of the bench-
ends of *Chedzoy* is a capital " M." (Queen Mary), surmounted by
a crown, and bearing the date 1539. In the interesting church
of *Clapton-in-Gordano* are plain benches of very early type
(147). At *Crowcombe*, where one of the ends is dated 1534,
there is much excellent design in foliage and even in figures ;
note the spirited design of two men killing a dragon, a grotesque
of foliage proceeding from the mouth of a large human head, and
a pair of mermen from the ears (146). *Curry Rivel* has a large
number of good bench-ends, chiefly of tracery ; there are also
several Passion symbols, and a remarkable one of the Ascension.
One of the beautifully carved bench-ends at *Kingston* bears the
date 1522 on a shield ; the designs are mostly imitative of
foliage, but one has a pair of oxen yokes, and above them two
small stags (149). *Middlezoy* has some fifteenth century bench-
ends, chiefly of tracery. The interior of *Milverton* has a remarkable display of bench-ends of the days of Queen Mary ; the
kneeling figure of the queen appears several times, as well as
those of Cardinal Pole and Bishop Gardiner, also kneeling.
The arms of Henry VIII. are shown on an end near the pulpit.
Another remarkable one represents the two spies with the huge
bunch of grapes. The execution of them all is rather coarse
(151). *Monksilver* has some specially charming fifteenth century
traceried bench-ends and panelling (152). *Rimpton* has a large
number of bench-ends, *c.* 1500 ; they are chiefly carved with
tracery, but some bear the quaint monogram I.H.C. *Sampford
Brett* has several carved seat-ends ; one of them with a figure of a
lady is of some renown, as it is supposed to represent Florence
Wyndham, of whom the story is told that she was buried in a
trance, from which she was awakened by the efforts of the sexton
to steal her ring. There are a variety of bench-ends at *Spaxton*
of the sixteenth century ; two of them bear the respective dates
of 1536 and 1561. The most notable represents a fuller at his
work, with all the implements of his trade around him (156).
Stogumber has a delightful collection of early sixteenth century
seating (157). *Tintinhull* bench-ends are remarkable, inasmuch
as they mostly retain the hinged flap seats attached to them
(22). As to *Trent* bench-ends see Dorset, to which county
this parish has been transferred (92). The late bench-ends of
Trull are of great interest. At the west end of the north aisle, the
craftsman's name and date appear inscribed above some linenfold
panelling : " Simon Warman maker of these worke Ano Doie
1560. John Waye Clarke here." It is rather remarkable, con-

Trull, Somerset

F. S.

Trull, Somerset

W. P. W.

Spaxton, Somerset

W. P. W.

Spaxton, Somerset

G. J. G.

F. H. C.   Stogumber Somerset

F. H. C.   Stogumber, Somerset

sidering the state of the work, to find that five of the panels represent figures in a religious procession, namely (1) a crucifer ; (2) a man with a candle ; (3) a man with a reliquary ; and (4) and (5) two choristers with books (155). An exceptionally good bench-end, ejected from some unknown Somerset church, representing the doubting St Thomas, is in the private collection of Dr Philip Nelson, F.S.A. *Weston Zoyland's* beautiful bench-ends, with alternate poppy-heads, are well illustrated in Bury's " Ecclesiastical Wood Work." They are finely worked in late Perpendicular tracery of great variety. The manor was held by Glastonbury abbey, and on one of the seat-ends are the initials " R. B." (Richard Bere) ; he was the last but one of the abbots. In the nave of *White Staunton* there are some of the original bench-ends, carved after an unusual fashion ; they are apparently of the close of Henry VIII.'s reign. One of the narrow or front panels of the seats is an animal apparently intended for a brock or badger ; another of the wider ends has a diamond-shaped arrangement, probably intended for fretty, which was the armorial bearing of the Stauntons. The bench-ends of *Wraxall* differ from most of the Somerset examples, inasmuch as they are not square-headed but shaped at the top ; they somewhat resemble those of *Clevedon*. It is not to be supposed that these comments in any way exhaust the list of churches retaining more or less of the ancient sittings. Old bench-ends are also to be seen at Alford, Bagborough, South Barrow, Bicknoller, Brunton, West Buckland, Queen Camel, West Camel, Charlton Mackrell, Cheddar, Chewton Mendip, Clevedon, Old Cleeve, Corton Denham, Cothelstone, Creech St Michael, St Decuman, Donyatt, Dunster, Hatch Beauchamp, Hill Farrance, Ile Abbots, Limington, Lydeard St Lawrence, Lyng, Mells, Merriott, Moor, Mudford, Nettlecombe, Norton Fitzwarren, Oake, West Pennard, Pitminster, Portbury, East Quantoxhead, Sandford Orcas, Somerton, Stoke St Gregory, Taunton, Thornfalcon, Tintinhull, Wellow, and Winsham— forty-six in all.

Hitherto our notes have only been on nave or aisle benches or bench-ends ; but the remains of the stall work of the chancels also calls for enumeration : *North Cadbury*, which was made collegiate in 1427, has stalls each side of the quire. At *Butleigh* there are one or two misericord stalls. *Orchard Portman* has some carved stalls. At *Weston-in-Gordano* and at *Worle* there are some old misericord stalls. In the latter case only the stalls on the north side are ancient ; one of them has the initials " P.R.S." These latter stand for Richard Sprynge, prior of Woodspring and vicar of Worle, *c.* 1480.

Denardiston, Suffolk

F. J. A.

SUFFOLK

The county of SUFFOLK stands nearly at the top of the tree for the multiplicity and beauty of its pre-Reformation seating. Poppy-heads abound everywhere. Fressingfield comes first in the ornateness and completeness of its benches and bench-ends. Blythburgh, Dennington, Laxfield, Stowlangtoft, Ufford, Wingfield, and Woolpit are not far behind, whilst Norton has both aisles well filled with ancient seats. Brief comments shall now be made on all the more noteworthy examples in alphabetical order. *Aldham* has some well-carved fifteenth century bench-ends with poppy-headed finials. The like may be said of *Great Ashfield, Great Barton,* and *Bedingfield.* At *Bildeston* a certain amount of old work remains in the stalls which were renewed in 1883, and in the seats of the nave and aisle renewed in 1886. There are some well-carved stalls and also open seats with poppy-heads at *Brandon.* The chancel of *Buxhall* retains two fifteenth century oak-panelled benches, carved with the arms of the Copinger and Harris families.

The noble old church of *Blythburgh* deserves a paragraph to itself wherein to tell of its ancient seating. In the chancel are a set of stalls with re-turned ends, with the Apostles in niches on the front panels; they are very well executed on a small scale, and the study of their respective emblems is quite interesting (164). On the poppy-headed standards are the quartered arms of Swillington and Ross. These stalls, which are quite unsuitable for a large quire, were most unfortunately moved here from the north chapel during a restoration of last century by Mr Street. But the most interesting of all the old woodwork is the array of old oak benches in the nave; they are coeval with the present church, *c.* 1475. The finials of the standards of many of the benches are most remarkable, and consist of human figures, several of a somewhat grotesque though speaking character. A set of seven are undoubtedly intended to personify the Seven Deadly Sins; they are boldly conceived, and represented with some skill and ingenuity. It is impossible to mistake Sloth or Hypocrisy. Sensuality was cut off at a comparatively recent period. The set of the Seasons, an attractive subject, is less original. These old seats, though they have such elaborately carved ends, were originally backless.

At *Charsfield* some of the old fifteenth century seats remain with poppy-head finials. At *Chediston* there are four old benches of this character, and there are others at *Combs.*

Ufford, Suffolk

T. B.

Chevington has some old oak seats; the standards have poppy-head finials; a few of the benches are carved with Renaissance designs. At *Cookley* there are some good panels to the stalls and figures on the bench-ends. The Perpendicular tracery in front of the quire stalls at *Dalham* is partly old and partly a reproduction of 1867. Some late fifteenth century benches remain at *Darsham* with traceried ends and poppy-head finials. *Debenham* has good panelled stalls with poppy-headed finials. *Denardiston* has some good stalls in

C. F. N.

Passion Bench, Fressingfield

the quire with well-carved misericords; the nave is fitted with open fifteenth century benches, having plain standards, but quaint animals on the finials and shoulders (159). *Dennington* has a wealth of handsome late fifteenth century benches with beautifully carved backs; the standards are all poppy-headed and enriched with tracery and set patterns (166). At *South Elmham All Saints* there are a few old open benches with the usual poppy-heads. *Elmswell* has some old seats with fifteenth century wide traceried standards surmounted by good poppy-heads. There are a few old benches at *Exning* showing linen-

Fressingfield, Suffolk

Fressingfield, Suffolk

fold panels on the ends. In the quire of *Framsden* there are some well-carved old seats, and others in the nave, the latter with poppy-heads. *Freckenham* has some excellent fifteenth century benches with plain standards surmounted by good poppy-heads; one of the finials has the clever figure of a lady kneeling at a desk telling her beads (165).

Fressingfield also well merits a distinctive paragraph, for the church is better filled throughout with excellent fifteenth century benches than any other church in the kingdom (162). The poppy-heads are exceptionally fine. The height of the fine

G. G. B.

Blythburgh, Suffolk

standards is 3 ft. 10 in., including the poppy-heads, and the greatest breadth is 1 ft. 1½ in. The height of the poppy-heads alone is 1 ft. 1½ in. All the standards are well carved after a diversity of designs. Two of the shoulder figures here represented are respectively those of St Peter and St Paul. The fronts and backs of the benches have also wavy traceried designs. The back of the last bench on the south side of the nave has the emblems of St Peter, St Paul, St Andrew, etc., within quatrefoils. On the back bench, locally known as the "Passion Bench," the subjects are as follows: (1) Cock crowing; (2) the buffet and the jug of vinegar; (3) I.H.C.; (4) scourging pillar, cords, and scourges; (5) the cross, crown of thorns, and nails; (6) the spear

F. H. C.

Dennington, Suffolk

J. F. E.

Freckenham, Suffolk

and sponge ; (7) the hammer, pincers, and ladder ; (8) the seam-less coat and diceboard.[1]

Frostenden has some excellent late fifteenth century bench and quire stall ends, with large poppy-heads ; there are also exceptionally good bench-ends at *Grandisburgh* and *Hackeston*. At *Hadleigh* the rude carving on a seat angle of the wolf with St Edmund's head is noteworthy (169). A few good old seats remain at *Hemingstone* and *Hitcham*. There are remains of old seat carving worked up into the new pewing of *Hundon*. In the

F. B.

Dennington, Suffolk

chancel of *Hunston* there are two fifteenth century bench-ends with well-carved poppy-heads. There is very little ancient seating left in the several old churches of *Ipswich*, but at St Mary-le-Tower the old misericord seats have been refixed as stalls, but the relief carved standards are all new ; there are also some delicately traceried panels on the back of a bench at St Margaret's. Some of the old stalls of *Lavenham* have

[1] The above are illustrated in Mr Francis Bond's " Dedications," pp. 284-289.

curiously carved misericords. At *Laxfield* there are some fine bench-ends, of like date with those of Fressingfield, *c.* 1480. *Mettingham* has a few carved stalls, and *Moulton* some good oak benches in the nave ; the remains of old seating is also noteworthy at *Nedging* and *Newbourne.* The aisles of *Norton* are nearly filled with old benches, some of which have finely carved poppy-heads and figures, and the chancel is remarkable for its eight misericords of the fourteenth century. In the chancel of *Otley* are some beautiful benches on which are the

C. F. N.

Stowlangtoft, Suffolk

letters " Prepare." There are some good benches with poppy-heads in the south aisle of *Rattlesden*, and further good benches at *Great Redisham* and *Redlingfield*, whilst at *Ringsfield* some old carved seating is worked up in the new benches of the nave. *Shelley* has some fine bench-ends ; in the chancel they bear, in front of the poppy-heads, the arms of Finlay quartering Thorpe. The richly carved stall work of the noble church of *Southwold*, immediately within the screen, is original, and only slightly repaired. There are four stalls with misericords, and three re-turned stalls facing east on each side. Some good fourteenth century stalls are retained in the chancel of *Stonham Aspall*. The fine and most interesting church of *Stowlangtoft* abounds in a glorious profusion of richly carved seating both in

Woolpit, Suffolk

Woolpit, Suffolk

nave and chancel, as can be far better realised from the plates than by any amount of letterpress. The figures of a priest reading, on the summit of one of the stalls, is strikingly executed (12). The bench-ends and backs of the seats in the body of the church

Wingfield, Suffolk

C. E. N.

Hadleigh, Suffolk

F. S. A.

22

are, with the exception of those of the Wiggenhalls in Norfolk,
the finest in England (167). The work seems to date from the
third quarter of the fourteenth century ; a local tradition, told
me in the 'seventies of last century, makes out that all this woodwork was a thank-offering from the squire and rector for pre-
serving their respective households from the horrors of the
Black Death. Some of the old misericord stalls remain in the
church of St Gregory, *Sudbury*. There are good carved benches
remaining at *Tostock* ; among the animals represented are the
cockatrice and unicorn. *Tuddenham St Martin* retains several
seats with rich panelling and well-carved poppy-heads. *Ufford*
is another of Suffolk's grand examples of splendid old seating
of fifteenth century date ; the poppy-heads are flanked by pairs
of small animals ; the plate speaks for itself (161). There is
also good work in the chancel. The bench-ends at *Westleton*
are considered to be Elizabethan. *Wingfield* can boast of the
survival of some good poppy-headed benches in the nave, and
of good stalls in the quire with panelled fronts (169). *Woolpit*
is yet another instance of the splendid Suffolk treatment of the
seating ; the date is early fifteenth century (168). It is quite
impossible, on account of space, to do more than give a list
of other Suffolk churches, which we believe to be fairly exhaus-
tive, wherein more or less remains of ancient seating can be
detected. But it must be noted that in some cases the remnants
may have disappeared or been swept away by rampant restorers,
for our notes of very frequent church visits in Suffolk reach
back to 1869. Aldeburgh, Aldringham, Aspall, Athelington,
Bacton, Badley, Barking, Barnardiston, Barrow, Barton Hill,
Great Bealings, Bentley, Blundeston, Bradfield St George,
Bramfield, Brockley, Bromefield, Bruisyard, St James' church,
Bury St Edmunds, Carlton, Cavendish, Chevington, Cockfield,
South Cave, Cowling, Cratfield, Culpho, Ellough, Elveden, Eriswell,
Felixstowe, Finningham, Gazeley, Gedding, Gislingham, Hartest,
Hasketon, Haughley, Hawstead, Henley, Hornington, Kedington,
Kettleburgh, Knettishall, Langham, Lawshall, Mellis, Mickfield,
Monk Eleigh, Monk Soham, Nowton, Occold, Parham, Posling-
ford, Preston, Risby, Rougham, Rushmere St Andrews, Shotti-
sham, Stansfield, Stanton All Saints, Stoke-by-Nayland, Stow-
market, Stradishall, Syleham, Thorington, Thorndon, Troston,
Ubbeston, Walsham-le-Willows, Wantisden, Wattisfield, Great
Wenham, Westhall, Wetheringsett, Wordwell, Great Wratting,
Little Wratting, Wyverstone, and Yaxley (eighty in all). In
Dr Philip Nelson's collection of old oak is a remarkable finial
to a bench-end from a Suffolk church, representing a man apparently playing the bagpipes and holding a nondescript animal.

SURREY

In the county of SURREY there is but little pre-Reformation seating left in the churches. Dunsfold is remarkable for the retention of plain massive benches, with good mouldings at the ends, of the exceptionally early date of *c.* 1290. Chancel stalls with misericords are to be found, as will be seen from the following notes, in six churches, pre-Reformation seating or benches in at least a score other churches. It will be best to briefly discuss them in alphabetical order. The greater part

G. C. D.

Dunsfold, Surrey

of the oak seating of *Alfold* is sixteenth century; the bench-ends are plain and spear-headed, but with a moulded capping. The quire stalls of *Beddington,* with their misericords, are good examples of fifteenth century work; the seven stalls on the south side, and the three western ones on the north side, are original. The stalls are of the normal type with semicircular moulded backs and elbow cappings; two of the old stalls on the north have monograms on the elbow pieces. In the vestry of *Capel* church a number of carved pew doors of seventeenth century date are worked up into a cupboard. At *Chiddingfold,* among the manifold changes of 1870, a few old seventeenth century seats were worked in with the new scheme of pewing;

in the vestry is preserved one of much earlier date with scrolled tops to the ends, possibly *c.* 1290, like those of the neighbouring church of Dunsfold. In the nave of *Dunsfold* are about a dozen solid old benches, about the close of the thirteenth century, and therefore of exceptional interest ; the parallel design of the top of the standards is quaint, said to resemble a pair of cow's horns with balls on the tips. In the vestry is part of a graceful fleur-de-lis finial of a quire stall of the same date, the only fragment remaining (171). At *Effingham* there remains an old bench-end with a fleur-de-lis finial, and part of another, both of fifteenth century date ; they have served as copies for the modern chancel seats. Among the museum-like display of the small church of *Gatton*, which has been almost choked with a perfectly incongruous collection of church furniture from more than a dozen continental places such as Ghent, Rouen, Louvain, and Nuremberg, brought here by Lord Monson in 1834, may be noted various portions of foreign quire stalls. A singularly unhappy restoration of *Horley* church in 1881-82 brought about the destruction of a good number of old seats, as well as of a lofty manorial pew of the Fenner family, dated 1654. At *Horne* a considerable quantity of sixteenth century oak panelling from ancient seating has been reused in the backs of the modern varnished deal pews during a bad restoration of 1880. On each side of the screen at *West Horsley* are re-turned stalls of early sixteenth century date. On the south side of the quire of *Lingfield*, made collegiate in 1480, are some fine stalls with good misericords, bearing portraits, arms, and badges of the families of Cobham and Bardolf. On the elbow of one of the stalls is a remarkable man's head. In the chancel of *Nutfield* there is a seat made up from two old bench-ends with poppy-heads, of early sixteenth century date. The fittings of *Ockham* are modern, except for a pair of early fourteenth century stall arms, belonging to a set of stalls of unknown origin; they were worked into seats, one on each side of the chancel. The nave of *Pyrford* still retains its late fifteenth century seating, with square panelled ends and moulded cappings. At *Thursley* there are some small remains of plain fifteenth century seats, worked in with new material in the chancel. Some ancient benches of the first half of the fourteenth century, formerly in the nave of *Witley*, were moved at the last restoration into the north chapel. There are some old stalls with misericords in the quire of *Worplesdon*, but they are mixed with modern work.

In the archiepiscopal chapel of *Croydon* attached to the palace, the extant buildings of which show traces of work extending from the days of Archbishop Courtenay (1381-96) down to those of Archbishop Juxon (1660-64), the old stall work is of exceptional beauty and interest.

SUSSEX

SUSSEX does not stand high among counties renowned for the amount or beauty of their mediæval seating. As to the quire stall with traceried canopies and misericords, those of Chichester, both in the cathedral and at St Mary's Hospital, have been already fully treated in Mr Bond's volume of the English Church Art Series. There is excellent stall work at *Etchingham, c.* 1346, and later work (restored) of the same century in *Arundel* chancel. The other remains of later old stalls will be mentioned in the following alphabetical summary list of Sussex's pre-Reformation seating. At *Alfriston* there is some small remnant of stall work, *c.* 1400. The early Perpendicular stalls and misericords at *Bosham* have quite recently, for some unknown reason, been removed from the chancel. Some early fifteenth century stalls and misericords are still to be seen in the chancel of *Broadwater.* At *Burpham* and *Burton* there is some stall work of a later date. *Climping* has some benches, *c.* 1381, and *Cold Waltham* sixteenth century seating. The nave of the small church of *Didling* is almost entirely filled with late thirteenth century seating, benches, curbs, and all complete. It also has some good plain seating, *c.* 1450, the standards of which are supported by shallow buttresses. *Kirdford* has some fifteenth century benches, and *East Lavant* some stall work earlier in the same century. *Mayfield* church retains the remains not only of the chancel screen but of the carved quire stalls beyond it, *c.* 1425. *Poynings* has some remnants of fifteenth century stall work, and *East Preston* some sixteenth century seating. There is a little stall work in *Rye's* great church of early fifteenth century date, and plain seating at *Rogate* of the early sixteenth century. The earliest seating in the county is at *Slindon* church; the plain and very substantial benches, the standards of which are finished off with embryo poppy-heads, cannot be later than the close of the thirteenth century (174). The date assigned to certain old benching retained at the churches of *Singleton, Sutton,* and *Tortington* by Mr P. M. Johnston, is *c.* 1420. The chancel of *West Tarring* still retains some stalls and misericords *c.* 1400. It is curious that, for so large a county, and one, moreover, that has always been so extensively wooded, the above list of old church seatings should be so meagre. But it must be remembered how strong, for two or three centuries, was the prejudice in favour of cosy pews in preference to open benches. Then, too, even of late years, the love of uniformity has brought about the ejection of the sturdy and often well-matched and enriched benches in favour of whole rows of precisely similar seats of sticky pitch

G. C. D.

Slindon, Sussex

pine. We can remember the disappearance of at least five such sets of good benches out of Sussex churches within four or five years, and to our list Mr P. M. Johnston has added the churches of Ford and Rustington, both of which, until recently, had fourteenth century seating. Seventeenth century pewing still exists here and there, as at *Botolphs*, *Mayfield*, and *Sedlescombe*.

WARWICKSHIRE

The remains of early seating are not remarkable or extensive in the fascinating county of WARWICK; they chiefly consist of stall work in old collegiate and other churches. The old collegiate church of *Astley* has some remains of the original quire stalls, with painted figures and scrolls. *Aston* (Birmingham) church, rebuilt last century, has some stall work from St Margaret's, Leicester. There are some remains of early seating at *Aston-Cantlow*, *Baddesley Clinton*, and *Coughton*. Previous to restoration in 1872, *Bonnington* possessed several substantial but plain fifteenth century benches. The old Drapers' chapel on the north side of the great church of St Michael's, *Coventry*, is enclosed with screen work and contains thirteen misericord stalls; there is also some surviving stall work in the church of the Holy Trinity of the same city. In the church of *Dunchurch* there are three fifteenth century square-topped bench ends reset in modern oak stalls; one of them bears the arms of the Isle of Man. The collegiate church of *Knowle* retains in the quire six of the fifteenth century misericord stalls on the north side, and five on the south. The woodwork of the quire stalls of *Lapworth* is formed from the unhappily destroyed rood-screen. At *Morton Bagot*, *Oxhill*, and *Preston Bagot* we noted some remains of old seats a few years ago. Old benches also disappeared from *Salford Priors* after a too rigorous restoration of 1874. Bloxam names the interesting little church of *Shotswell* as an example of "dignified fittings of pew work of early fifteenth century, if not of the fourteenth." At *Snitterfield* the ends of the quire stalls are carved with Perpendicular tracery; one of them bears the arms of England and France quarterly, with dragon and greyhound as supporters, which were borne by Henry VIII. as well as Henry VII. But in the place of the crown of England is a mitre, probably a clumsy mistake of the carver. The front of the stalls bear Renaissance pilasters with figures of a bishop and a prior, the latter being probably intended for a prior of St Sepulchre's, Warwick, to whom this church belonged. In the fine cruciform church of *Solihull* there are some remnants of old stall work, and also at *Stratford-on-Avon*. Bloxam (ii. 32) illustrates the plain but well-moulded benches with elbowed ends of *Tysoe* church, evidently of fifteenth century date. The seats of the wonderful Beauchamp chapel, on the south side of St Mary's, *Warwick*, are of splendidly carved oak, with arms formed of bears, griffins, and lions; they were erected between 1444 and

1464. There are some remains of old seating at *Wolfhamcote, Wootton Wawen,* and *Wormleighton.*

WILTSHIRE

The churches of WILTSHIRE make but a poor display so far as old seating is concerned. There used to be a fair amount of interesting and substantial work of this description, including many poppy-head finials, up and down the county ; but between 1840 and 1880 restoring architects, including men of repute in their profession, played sad havoc with the interiors of many of the Wiltshire churches. An octogenarian ecclesiologist has sent us a list of eleven churches wherein he remembers seeing good thirteenth and early sixteenth century benches, all now no more. " Reseated throughout in pitch pine " is the usual conclusion to restoration summaries. We content ourselves with citing the " Gentleman's Magazine " account of *Bremhill* church in 1840 : " There are several varieties of oak carving in the panel work of the seats, which exhibit their original standards, though blended with modern additions." At *Britford* church, before its restoration by Street in 1873, there were many portions of old thirteenth century seats with poppy-heads. The restorer incorporated some which he considered the best in the new fittings of the chancel. One has a sprig of a tree issuing from a tun, a rebus which is probably intended for Ashton. A few old open benches were ejected from the church of *Castle Eaton* at a Butterfield restoration. *Crudwell* still retains some good carved bench-ends. At *Durnford* there are square-headed traceried fifteenth century bench-ends to the seats throughout, except a few plain ones at the west end ; they were somewhat restored in 1883. In the chancel of *Highworth* three of the fifteenth century stalls, with their misericords, remain. The late fifteenth century stalls in the quire of the fine and interesting church of *Mere* were originally in two sets of three each, but this arrangement has been altered ; they all had misericords, one of a Tudor rose and leaves. The one of a fox with foliage is new. The desk fronts on both sides are original, but badly recut and refaced. The two poppy-headed ends are also original ; the west ends are only traceried, but each of the two has a shield, suspended from a hand bearing the arms of Kymer. The seats of the nave are formed out of the original ones of Carolean date, made by " Walter the Joyner of Maiden Bradley," between 1638 and 1641, when they cost £86. 11s. 10d. ; the accounts show that the men and women sat apart. In the abbey church of *Malmesbury* there are oak seats with linenfold panelling ; the ends or standards have scroll work with poppy-head finials. At *Minety* there is good carving on some of the seating. The remains of stall work at *Salisbury* cathedral are fragmentary. The oak seats in the nave of *Stanton Fitzwarren* were formerly in Chiseldon church, but have been reconstructed. They were cast out of the latter church in 1893. The prayer desk of *Steeple Langford* is made of well-carved old seat-ends of fifteenth century date. One represents an angel holding a shield with the three nails ; the other a nondescript animal with eagle's head and wings, but a beast's body.

WORCESTERSHIRE

WORCESTERSHIRE has a fair share in the remains of ancient seating. Stalls and misericords have been fully discussed in other volumes, but it may be briefly summarised here that they exist at Great Malvern (24, *c.* 1400), Little Malvern, Pershore (fragmentary), Ripple, Worcester cathedral (fourteenth century). A summarised account of this shire, which appeared in the "Gentleman's Magazine" for 1862, states that the naves of Chaddesley-Corbett, Great Comberton, Cropthorne, Elmley Castle, Overbury, and Strensham were filled with old open benches. At Overbury, Bredon, Sedgebourne, North Piddle and Cropthorne the bench-ends had carved tracery, but the rest were plain with moulded top rails. The ends at Sedge-bourne and Elmley Castle had plain poppy-head finials. Unfortunately these old benches have in one or two cases disappeared since 1862 ; restoration fever raged somewhat severely in Worcestershire during the second half of last century. We now proceed to give a few particulars in alphabetical order of those churches retaining old seating of various dates. A pew in the south transept of *Bretforton* church is made up with elaborately carved panels, one of which is dated 1615, but others are earlier. *Broadway* has a considerable amount of fifteenth century carved work among the pewing. In the seating of *Claines* is some early seventeenth century panelling. Many of the nave seats of *Cropthorne* have late fifteenth century traceried ends with shallow buttresses, and similar fronts or backs by the passages. The nave walls of *Doverdale* are panelled all round with seventeenth century woodwork, chiefly from old destroyed pews. Amid the pewing of the south aisle of *Elmley Castle* church are four turned legs, which probably pertained to a 1637 altar-table mentioned in the Churchwardens' Accounts ;

23

there are also four standards for misericord stalls in the chancel. The church further contains a large number of sixteenth century benches with moulded rails. At *Hampton* various pieces of carved early Jacobean work from the ends of discarded seats have been used up for a reredos or for panelling the east end of the chancel. A costly restoration by Street, in 1858, of *Hanley Castle* church resulted in the "introduction of open benches reproduced from ancient examples," but we believe that none of the old ones are now extant. At *Haddington* certain linenfold panels from seat-ends have been reused in front of the quire stalls. *Harrington* retains several Elizabethan open seats in the nave, dated 1582 ; they bear texts from Scripture on the backs and ends. Each side of the chancel of *Little Malvern* has five stalls with carved elbow rests ; one of them represents two pigs feeding out of a bowl, but all the misericord bosses have been cut away. At *Middle Littleton* the heavy nave seats are mostly of fifteenth century date, with moulded top rails and traceried panel ends, and fronts or backs adjoining a passage ; one pew has linenfold panels. *South Littleton* has a fair number of fifteenth century seats in the nave, with heavy moulded cappings and tracery on the ends. Some of the oak seats of *Oddingley* are made up with reused seventeenth century woodwork. At *Overbury* the seats (much restored) are all late fifteenth century, the top rails are elaborately moulded, but otherwise quite plain ; one, however, has linenfold panels on the two ends. In the small church of *Pendock* most of the old benches remain, *c.* 1500 ; some of the ends have linenfold panels. At *Ripple* there are fourteen fine stalls of the fifteenth century, with moulded elbow rests and good misericords. There are a few original fifteenth century bench-ends remaining at *Sedgebarrow*. At *Tredington* there are many fifteenth century bench-ends and pew-fronts with traceried panels and moulded rails. The nave seating of *Wickhamford* is high eighteenth century pews, but in the ends and doors are framed an interesting series of carved panels, *c.* 1500, chiefly linenfold patterns of different types, some of the more elaborate having vine leaves and grapes at both top and bottom. The pew next the pulpit has six richly carved panels of late fifteenth century date ; these, and some further panels on the clerk's desk, are said to have been brought from France about 1840. A plain bench-end, but with a curiously moulded upper part, in the small church of *Warndon*, is illustrated in the "Builder" for 1851, p. 110. We believe it to be of early fourteenth century date.

YORKSHIRE

In the vast area of YORKSHIRE it is specially difficult, as has been the case throughout most of the preceding counties, to distinguish with any degree of certainty between seating of pre-Reformation or post-Reformation date during the sixteenth century. On the whole it seems best to discuss briefly the pewing generally for all three Ridings in alphabetical order, from the comparatively few early examples, such as the grand ones at Hemingborough and Wensley, down to the close of the seventeenth century.

At *Arksey* (W. R.) is a certain amount of good seventeenth century pewing. *Aysgarth* (N. R.) suffered a most disastrous and ignorant restoration ; it much spoilt the woodwork of the chancel, which was brought here from Jervaulx abbey. The reading-desk, of good fifteenth century carving, is formed from old stalls, and bears the rebus, a hazel tree and tun of William de Hesleton, who was elected abbot of Jervaulx in 1475. *Barnoldswick* (W. R.) has some ancient stall work with the arms of Kirkstall abbey ; also a good deal of seventeenth century pewing. At *Bolton by Bolland* (W. R.) there is also some seventeenth century pewing. The grand Perpendicular church of *Bolton Percy* has six re-turned stalls in the chancel, and also some good Jacobean seating. *Burneston* (N. R.) has some handsomely carved and somewhat imposing Carolean pews in the nave, erected in 1627. At *Carlton Husthwaite* (N. R.) the pews in the nave appear to be coeval with the pulpit, which is dated 1678. Four old poppy-heads are to be noted on the bench-ends in the chancel of *South Cowton* (N. R.). The extraordinary elevated Milbank pew in the north aisle of *Croft* (N. R.) is noted in Chapter III. In the south chapel of *Darfield* (W. R.) there is an old pew with the initials " T. B." and " R. B.," and the arms of Bosvile of Newhall twice repeated. At *Darrington* (W. R.) there are twelve late fifteenth century bench-ends, six at the west end of each aisle. There is much seventeenth century pewing at *Dent* (W. R.), and dates extending from 1619 to 1693 may be noted. At *Drax* (W. R.) there are a number of advanced sixteenth century bench-ends throughout the church, exhibiting in their carvings a transition from Gothic to Renaissance. The arms of Babthorpe of Drax may be noticed ; also the instruments of the Passion, together with the Five Wounds, the Prince of Wales's feather, a thistle, and a Tudor rose. The church of *Ecclesfield* (W. R.) displays some good seating, as well as screen work, in both the north and south chapels, *c.* 1530. One of the bench-ends bears Wombwell impaling Arthington, and another Wombwell impaling Wentworth. In the chancel of the interesting church of *Fishlake*

F. H. C.   Hemingborough, Yorks.

F. H. C.   Hemingborough, Yorks.

(W. R.) is a fragment of pewing dated "*Anno domini* 1616." At *Guiseley* (W. R.) is an old box pew with initials, in the south chapel, of seventeenth century date. *Halifax* (W. R.) retains three old stalls with misericords, which serve as sedilia, and also six

Hemingborough, Yorks.

F. H. C.

re-turned stalls with misericords at the west end of the chancel.
There is also a grand display of fine Jacobean carving. In the
south chapel of *Hatfield* there are some fifteenth century traceried
seat-ends ; also one dated 1622, with the initials " M. F. T. S."
One of the glories of the noble church of *Hemingborough* (E. R.)
is its interesting display of woodwork. In addition to the
screen work, there are seventeen stalls in the chancel with
poppy-heads at the ends, *c.* 1511, and a fine series of restored
square-headed bench-ends in the nave. Some of these latter
are carved with good Perpendicular tracery ; one shows a
grotesque fool's head, with a youth's bust below ; another one
a clown's head, with a dragon below ; and a third the arms
of Babthorpe. In the vestry are three panels of grotesque
animal forms, remarkably well executed (181). At *Husthwaite*
(N. R.) are a number of seventeenth century pews. *Kirkby*
Hill (N. R.) has some fifteenth century bench-ends and poppy-
heads, which have been copied in the newer work. *Kirkburton*
(W. R.) retains a good deal of seventeenth century pewing.
Kirkby Malham (W. R.) has some fine old pewing of early
seventeenth century date throughout the church ; some of the
best are at the east end of the north aisle, one of which is dated
1619, and another 1631. *Kirkby Ravensworth* (N. R.) has
a fragment of old woodwork under the tower, dated 1639.
There is some old carved woodwork, rudely executed, incorporated in several of the pews at *Leake* (N. R.). In the chancel
are two carved sixteenth century bench-ends, with remarkable
deeply under-cut poppy-heads ; the one on the north bears the
arms of the See of York, whilst that on the south has a rebus
of Hampton, and the date 1519 ; each of them has a grotesque
monster and an illegible inscription. It is not possible, in this
place, to do more than just mention the notable woodwork of
the well-known church of *St John's, Leeds* (1631-34). There
were some sixteenth century bench-ends in the little church
of *Marton-on-the-Trent* (N. R.). *Rotherham* (W. R.) chancel
has late fifteenth century stalls and seating, showing the
arms of Wombwell and the Shrewsbury Talbot ; the poppy-
heads terminate in figures. There are also old bench-ends in the
Jesus chapel ; one has the sacred monogram, two the name
Thomas Gurre, and the fourth Wombwell impaling Wentworth.
There are two heraldic bench-ends at *Sandal* (W. R.), showing
the Percy locket and crescent, and Percy impaling Frost, etc., together with the inscription : "*Orate pro bono statu Joselynny Pyrcy*
Armigery." Josceline Percy, youngest son of the fourth Duke of
Northumberland, married Margaret Frost, *c.* 1523 ; he died
1531. At *Sprotborough* (W. R.) there are sixteenth century

H. E. I.

H. E. I.

H. E. I.

H. E. I.

Wensley, Yorkshire

W. M.

Ripon Minster

re-turned stalls in the chancels, and also much old pewing in the body of the church, with grotesque carving on some of the doors. Ancient bench-ends are to be noted at *Thirsk* (N. R.), in the chancel and in the north and south aisles. At *Treeton* (W. R.) are the remains of early sixteenth century seating in the nave, inscribed "*Orate pro anima Magistri Willmi Holme quondam rectoris hujus ecclesie*"; he was instituted in 1513 ; there is a talbot on two of the bench-ends. There are some old stalls with misericords in the chancel of *Wakefield*; on the summit of the poppy-heads is the Savile owl. In the north chapel of *Wath-upon-Dearne* (W. R.) are five Elizabethan bench-ends bearing the arms of Savile, Fleming, and Charlesworth, together with this inscription: "Johne Savill caused this to be made the 19 da of September in the yere of our Lorde God 1576." *Woodkirk* (W. R.) has some good Perpendicular seating in the chancel; the poppy-heads have the initials "J. S." (John Savile), and terminate in a wheatsheaf. There are some good square-headed bench-ends, early sixteenth century, in the nave of *Woolley* (W. R.), several of which are heraldic.

Wensley (N. R.) richly merits a paragraph to itself. Space does not permit of any elaborate description of the far-famed monumental pew of Lord Bolton at the east end of the north aisle. Suffice it to say that though the front is quasi-classical, the back and sides formed part of the ground screen work of the Scrope parclose in Easby abbey. They were re-erected here after the dissolution, and, when perfect, must have composed a complete genealogy of the family. In the chancel are some strikingly beautiful chancel stalls with fine poppy-heads and heraldic beasts. They exhibit the arms of Scrope of Bolton and Tiptoft. Round all runs the following inscription: "*Henricus Richardson hujus ecclesie rector hos fecit sumptus* (anno) *Domini* MCCCCCXXVII. *Soli Deo honor et gloria*" (183). It would be foreign to the purport of these pages to enter into any account of the stall work of the two great minster churches of *Beverley* and *Ripon* ;[1] but it may be permitted to draw attention to the highly remarkable carvings on poppyheads in each of these minsters of an elephant with a howdah (184).

[1] Illustrated in "Stalls and Tabernacle Work," by Mr Francis Bond, pp. 3, 7, 14, 27, 63, 64, 65, 8, 60.

St David's Cathedral

Clynnog, N. Wales

WALES

WALES retains a few relics of early seating in her churches. The question of the stalls of the Welsh cathedrals has been discussed already in a previous volume of this series, but mention must be made of a fine stall standard with carved poppy-head from the quire of *St David's*, a cathedral which must prove a special joy to every architectural pilgrim (186).

The church of *Beaumaris*, Anglesey, has some interesting stalls with misericords; they are certainly older than its sixteenth century chancel, and were probably brought here from some suppressed religious house. The standard or bench-end of the present priest's stall in the chancel of *Beguildy*, Radnorshire, is somewhat rude and heavy; probable date, late thirteenth century. It was discovered beneath the chancel floor at a restoration of 1896. The church of *Caerwys*, Flint, has a handsomely carved pew door, dated 1687, and with the initials " W. H. M." It is surrounded by panels of old screen work. *Clynnog*, Carnarvonshire, a most interesting church, in addition to much older and valuable woodwork, has altar and stalls with misericords and desks of fifteenth century; the most remarkable of the poppy-head bench-ends is carved with a double-head eagle (186). The small church of *Disserth*, Radnorshire, has oak pews of diverse shapes and sizes; they bear a variety of inscriptions and dates, from 1666 to 1753. The church of *Gresford*, Denbighshire, retains all the original stalls and desks of the fifteenth century; the poppy-heads of the bench-ends are exceptionally fine. We reproduce one of the more remarkable with the erect Virgin (188). The cathedral-like church of St Mary, *Haverfordwest*, has a remarkably fine bench-end carved on the panel with St Michael killing a three-headed dragon; the finial is a well-developed poppy-head bearing the arms of England (the three lilies of France quartered with three lions of England) as used by Henry VIII., the whole surmounted by a coroneted mitre (189). At *Hawarden* (Flintshire) there is a particularly fine heraldic bench-end, which, together with some chancel seating, was the only part of the fittings saved from a fire of 29th October 1857. The poppy-head finial bears on each side a pelican with raised wings amidst vine tendrils and grapes; on the one side the bird bears a scroll inscribed " In Domino confido," and on the other a scroll inscribed " Spero in Domino." Below are the beautifully executed arms of York, of York Hall, quartering those of

Gresford

Buerton and Capenhurst. The bench is now attached to the
reading-desk, together with a new bench-end bearing the arms
of Glynne. Its date is 1520, and it was doubtless executed by

Haverfordwest

the same craftsman who carved the panels at Eastham, Cheshire (62). In the vestry of *Llanelidan*, Denbighshire, are a few Jacobean carved pew doors. The single-chambered church of *Llanfihangel Helygen*, Radnorshire, retains its rude and primitive arrangements, including old square pews and plain benches ; the latter are certainly pre-Reformation. In *Llangynhafel* church is a kind of eleventh century oak settle, serving as sedilia ; it was formerly in Llanbedr old church. There are also two Jacobean pews. The church of *Llanwnys*, Denbighshire, has a panelled dado carved with subjects from the bestiaries ; they appear to have been originally parts of fifteenth century bench-ends or other seating. The north wall of the chancel has some plain panelling, originally seating, inscribed " John Richards, vicar, Llanyns, March 26, 1613." A fragment of a stall was found in the church of *Meliden*, Flintshire, in 1885, supporting the pulpit ; enough remained to show that it was like those of Clynnog. The church of *Montgomery* has some good carved stall work with carved misericords, and good poppy-heads to the standards. All these, together with the well-proportioned screen, are said to have been brought from the neighbouring abbey of Chirbury, to which this church was appendant at the time of the dissolution. The walls of the tower of *Nerquis*, Flint, have been recently lined with the woodwork preserved from destroyed pews.

BIBLIOGRAPHY

"History of Pues." Cambridge Camden Society. 3rd edition. 1843.

"History of Pews," 2 vols. Major Heales. 1872.

"History of Seat Reservation in Churches." "Archæologia," LIII., ix. W. H. Hardy. 1892.

"English Church Furniture," pp. 248-300. Cox and Harvey. 1905.

"Early Churchwardens' Accounts," pp. 136-194. Rev. Dr Cox. 1913.

"Curious Church Gleanings," pp. 138-162. W. Andrews. 1895.

"Church Lore Gleanings," pp. 184-195. T. F. Thiselton Dyer. 1891.

"The Ecclesiologist." Cambridge Camden Society. 1842-65.

"The Ecclesiastical and Architectural Topography of Beds., Berks., Bucks., Cambs., Oxon., and Suffolk." Seven parts. Parker. 1848-55.

"The Architecture and History of the Churches of the Archdeaconry of Northampton." Parker. 1846-48.

"History and Architecture of Churches around Peterborough." W. B. Sweeting. 1868.

"Notes on Parish Churches." Sir Stephen Glynne, Bart., compiled between 1823 and 1873.

    Kent, printed in 1877.

    Lancashire, printed in 1893.

    Cheshire, printed in 1894.

    East Riding, Yorks., printed in 1894.

"County Churches," edited by Rev. Dr Cox. G. Allen & Co. 1910-13. *Cambridgeshire*, G. E. Evelyn-White; *Cornwall*, Dr Cox; *Cumberland and Westmorland*, Dr Cox; *Isle of Wight*, Dr Cox; *Norfolk*, 2 vols., Dr Cox; *Nottinghamshire*, Dr Cox; *Suffolk*, 2 vols., T. H. Bryant; *Surrey*, J. E. Morris.

"Stalls and Tabernacle Work"; also "Misericords." Francis Bond. 1910.

"Victoria County Histories—Beds., Hants, Lancs., Surrey, Sussex."

"Gothic Ornament," 2 vols. J. K. Colling. 1848-50.

"Gothic Details," 2 vols. J. K. Colling. 1852.

"Ancient English Architecture." J. Potter. 1857.

"Instrumenta Ecclesiastica." 1847.

"Remains of Ecclesiastical Woodwork." T. Talbot Bury. 1845.

"Gothic Wood Carving." Franklin A. Crollan. 1896.

"Reports of Monuments Commission for Bucks. and Herts."

Sketch Books of (1) "Spring Gardens," (2) "Architectural Association" (three series), and (3) "John O'Gaunt."

Also various volumes of *Builder*, *Builders' Journal*, *Architect*, *British Architect*, and *Building News*.

INDEX OF PLACES

The page number is printed in clarendon type where there is an illustration

INDEX OF PERSONS AND SUBJECTS

Printed at THE DARIEN PRESS, *Edinburgh.*

Church Art in England

A Series of Books edited by

FRANCIS BOND, M.A., F.G.S., Hon. A.R.I.B.A.

HUMPHREY MILFORD, OXFORD UNIVERSITY PRESS
LONDON, NEW YORK, TORONTO, MELBOURNE, & BOMBAY

SCREENS AND GALLERIES IN ENGLISH CHURCHES

Demy 8vo, containing 204 pages, with 152 Illustrations reproduced from Photographs and Drawings. Strongly bound in cloth. Price 6s. net ($2.40).

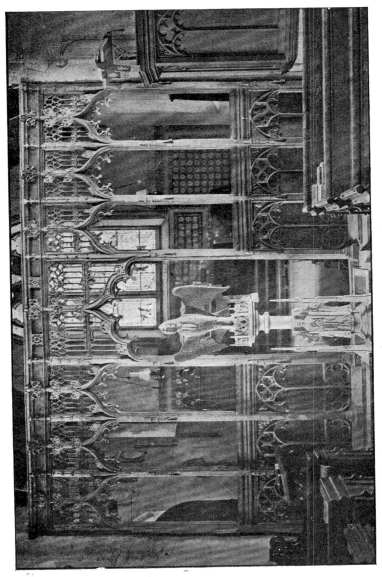

Screen in Scarning Church, Norfolk

New York Nation.—"It is not easy to praise too highly the simple and effective presentation of the subject and the interest of the book to all persons who care for ecclesiology or for decorative art."

Daily Graphic.—"Mr Bond has produced a work on our ecclesiastical screens and galleries which, like his larger work on the 'Gothic Architecture of England,' is

Screen in Holbeton Church

in the first degree masterly. His knowledge of his subject, exact and comprehensive, is compressed into a minimum amount of space, and illustrated by a series of photographs and measured drawings which render the work of permanent value."

Bulletin Monumental.—"Après avoir analysé, aussi exactement que possible, l'intéressant étude de M. Bond, nous devons le féliciter de nous avoir donné ce complément si utile à son grand ouvrage."

FONTS & FONT COVERS

Demy 8vo, containing 364 pages, with 426 Illustrations reproduced from Photographs and Measured Drawings. Strongly bound in cloth. Price 12s. net ($4.80).

Font at Stanton Fitzwarren

Font at Belton

PRESS NOTICE

Church Quarterly Review.—"It is most delightful, not only to indulge in a serious perusal of this volume, but to turn over its pages again and again, always sure to find within half a minute some beautiful illustration or some illuminating remark."

Font at Bodmin

BY FRANCIS BOND

Wood Carvings in English Churches
I. Misericords

Demy 8vo, containing 257 pages, with 241 Illustrations reproduced
from Photographs and Measured Drawings. Strongly bound in
cloth. Price 7s. 6d. net ($3.00).

Misericords at Stratford-on-Avon

SOME PRESS NOTICES

New York Herald.—"One of the quaintest, most fascinating, and at the same time most learned volumes that a reader would happen upon in a lifetime."

Antiquary.—"An authoritative, and at the same time delightful and instructive volume."

Church Times.—"An indispensable guide to the subject. The illustrations are worthy of all praise."

Yorkshire Post.—"Another of the valuable series of monographs on Church Art in England, and the most entertaining of all."

Misericord at Worcester

Misericord at Beverley Minster

Liverpool Courier.—"Another of the admirably written and illustrated art handbooks for which the author is famous."

Birmingham Post.—"This well illustrated volume is not only a valuable technical monograph, but also an important contribution to the history of social life and thought in the Middle Ages. Mr Bond's treatment of the subject is exceptionally charming and successful."

Outlook.—"Many there must be to whom Mr Bond's new book will be welcome. Into all the details of this varied and most puzzling subject he goes with thoroughness and a pleasant humour. The bibliography and indices, as in all the volumes in this series, are admirable."

Wood Carvings in English Churches
II. Stalls and Tabernacle Work, Bishops' Thrones, and Chancel Chairs

Demy 8vo, containing 154 pages, with 124 Illustrations reproduced from Photographs and Measured Drawings. Strongly bound in cloth. Price 6s. net ($2.40).

Stalls at Lancaster

PRESS NOTICE

La Chronique des Arts et de la Curiosité.—"Une illustration copieuse établie avec des soins tout documentaires ; des index ; une table par ordre chronologique, une autre par noms des lieux, viennent faciliter les recherches et permettre au lecteur de tirer bénéfice des vastes resources d'une érudition informée et sure."

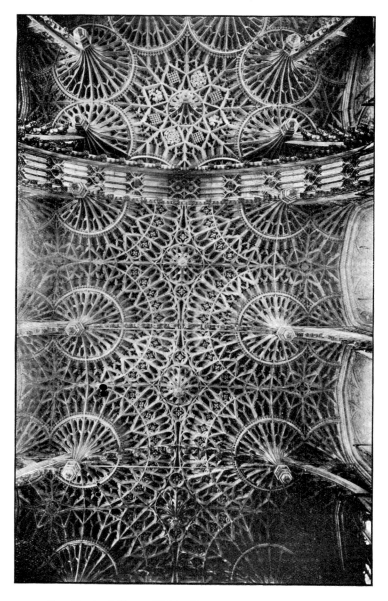

Fan Vault of Henry VII.'s Chapel in Westminster Abbey

VISITORS' GUIDE TO WESTMINSTER ABBEY

93 pages of text, abridged from the larger work on "Westminster Abbey."
Fcap 8vo, with 15 Plans and Drawings and 32 Photographic Illustrations.
Price 1s. net (40 c.).

Chapter House at Westminster

Dedications and Patron Saints of English Churches. Calendars. Ecclesiastical Symbolism. Saints and their Emblems

Demy 8vo, containing 359 pages, with 252 Illustrations.
Strongly bound in cloth.   Price 7s. 6d. net ($3.00).

THE main object of the book is to inquire into the dedications of the English churches, and to show the curious
ways which led to the popularity, or it may be the
unpopularity, of the various saints.   To aid in the identi-
fication of the saints represented in mediæval art very numerous
illustrations have been reproduced from stained glass, statuary
in wood, stone, and alabaster, ivories, brasses, bench ends,
wall paintings, illuminated manuscripts, and painted rood-
screens.   At the end will be found an alphabetical list,
with dates and emblems, of the saints commemorated in
English dedications, and another alphabetical list of the
emblems of the saints ; these two lists will be found of service
in visiting the picture galleries and stained glass of England
and the Continent.

SOME PRESS NOTICES

Morning Post.—"Mr Bond's indefatigable industry and gift of *flair* in ecclesiastical matters have found a wide scope in this fascinating field ; we have had as
much pleasure in reading it as he had in writing it.   It is the work of a true
enthusiast, and will greatly help the diffusion of a keener and more intelligent
interest in the visible and invisible antiquities of our innumerable ancient churches."

Yorkshire Observer.—"Out of the fulness of his learning the writer has made
this volume a most curious revelation of the wit, wisdom, superstition and romance of
the Middle Ages."

Times Literary Supplement.—"Mr Bond's previous works have dealt with
English ecclesiastical architecture and carving, with an elaboration of illustration and
description for which students a century hence will be profoundly grateful.   Readers
of the present book should be many, for it contains much that is delightful."

The Chancel of English Churches

The Altar, Reredos, Lenten Veil, Communion Table, Altar Rails, Houseling Cloth, Piscina, Credence, Sedilia, Aumbry, Sacrament House, Easter Sepulchre, Squint, Etc.

Demy 8vo, containing 275 pages, with 229 Illustrations. Strongly bound in cloth. Price 7s. 6d. net ($3.00).

SOME PRESS NOTICES

Daily Graphic.—"To the many admirable books he has written that others may share his informed delight in the treasures of our English churches, Mr Bond has added 'The Chancel of English Churches.'"

Scotsman.—"To the admirable series of richly illustrated volumes in which the author has sought to examine and exhibit the inexhaustible treasures in art and archæology of the English churches comes a worthy successor which deals with the altar and its accessories."

Guardian.—"Mr Bond has added yet another volume to his well-known and much-appreciated series of books on 'Church Art in England.' In common with the other books, it gives evidence of remarkable industry and very wide reading. But the special feature of the whole series is the wealth and admirable nature of the illustrations, the large majority of which are reproductions of special photographs."

Yorkshire Observer.—"It is because the parish church is so frequently full of historical survivals that one most cordially welcomes this noble series of monographs."

Builder.—"Another volume in the great series of works of reference which Mr Bond has already produced, and for which he has acquired a well-deserved reputation."

Building News.—"Another of the deeply interesting and scholarly volumes on English churches and their details, replete with reliable information, accurate in its logical conclusions, attractive in method of treatment, and profusely illustrated. . . . We have freely drawn on it to indicate the freshness and charm of Mr Bond's treatment of the subject and the permanent value and interest of his work."

BY H. B. WALTERS

Church Bells of England

Demy 8vo, containing 420 pages, with 170 Illustrations
reproduced from Photographs and Drawings. Strongly
bound in cloth. Price 7s. 6d. net ($3.00).

Times.—"It is by far the most complete work of its kind in existence and the most accurate . . . a treatise as readable as it is erudite."

Cross and Letters on Lincolnshire Bells (1423-1431)

Pulpits, Lecterns, and Organs

Demy 8vo, containing 239 pages, with 155 Illustrations. Strongly bound in cloth. Price 7s. 6d. net ($3.00).

SOME PRESS NOTICES

Times.—"A thoroughly enjoyable book, useful for both reading and reference."

Spectator.—"There are many and beautiful illustrations opposite almost every page, so well arranged with reference to the text that they add very greatly to the reader's instruction and pleasure."

Saturday Review.—"Dr Cox has brought to his study a wide and accurate knowledge of church life in mediæval England."

Westminster Gazette.—"With Dr Cox as guide the lover of old church furniture can spend delightful hours; and a perusal of this scholarly book will send many a reader to church interiors with a zest never felt before."

Pall Mall Gazette.—"It would be difficult to estimate our indebtedness to Dr Cox for the many excellent works on churches and church life which he has written. The last one, on a subject which has been greatly neglected, bears evidence once again to his painstaking thoroughness, and to that vast learning which has so often been used to correct the mistakes of amateurs and other unqualified disputants."

Church Quarterly.—"We think it in every way worthy of its author's reputation."

Guardian.—"This handsome volume, with its profusion of fine illustrations, will assuredly enlist the interest of all lovers of serious archæology."

Church Family Newspaper.—"Every page of this delightful volume grips the reader, and is calculated to arouse an intelligent interest in church lore. There are a large number of beautifully produced illustrations."

Builder.—" The book is useful and interesting, and is very clearly and well written."

Building News.—" The work before us is penned by the Rev. Dr J. Charles Cox, the author of many books on ecclesiological subjects, and it is marked by the painstaking accuracy and the wide range of scholarship associated with the author's name. The only monograph on pulpits hitherto published has been F. T. Dollman's ' Examples of Ancient Pulpits,' issued in 1849, and long since out of print."

British Architect.—" The author of this excellent volume on pulpits, lecterns, and organ cases, has a long list of publications to his credit, but perhaps none which would be more welcome to architects than this latest, which is full of interest from cover to cover, well produced, and of moderate price."

Scotsman.—" No book on Ancient English Pulpits has, it seems, seen the light since the appearance in 1849 of Mr Dollman's work, now long out of print as well as out of date. It was therefore high time that an experienced and indefatigable authority such as Dr Cox should take up and present to us, in the handsome and richly illustrated form of a volume of the ' Church Art in England ' series, this interesting branch of ecclesiology."

Yorkshire Post.—" If one had time to go carefully through the many books on English churches and church lore into which the Rev. Dr J. Charles Cox, F.S.A., has packed the researches of a lifetime, and to compile from them a list of the 'common mistakes' which he has corrected, it would be possible to make a highly entertaining volume. His latest book would lengthen the list considerably. It embraces a great chapter of church history which has not hitherto been so thoroughly dug over, and Dr Cox has discovered in it many relics of ancient practice and custom which are of much value, not alone as curiosities, but also for the light they throw upon the past."

Military Architecture in England During the Middle Ages

By A. Hamilton Thomson, M.A., F.S.A.

Demy 8vo, containing 406 pages, with 200 Illustrations reproduced from Photographs, Drawings, and Plans. Strongly bound in cloth. Price 7s. 6d. net ($3.00).

Bodiam : North Front and Gatehouse

SOME PRESS NOTICES

Church Times.—"Not only those who are specially interested in military architecture, but also everyone who desires, on visiting an ancient castle, to view it with intelligent appreciation, must needs add this work to his library."

Guardian.—"This volume at once steps into the position of a classic; it will be long before it is superseded."

English Historical Review.—"This monograph is compressed into about four hundred pages, and copiously illustrated, yet it contains a wealth of detail that could easily have been expanded into a much longer work. . . . Its author is not writing a guide to castles, but a history of military architecture; yet the work might usefully be taken as a guide to many of the castles described in it."

Country Life.—"The book could scarcely be bettered as a concise survey of a difficult and complex subject."

Journal des Savants. — "Le livre de M. Thomson sera . . . le bienvenu. Il le sera d'autant plus qu'il donne un aperçu très complet des transformations de l'architecture militaire outre-Manche depuis les temps les plus anciens. . . . Ce n'est pas seulement au point de vue anglais, c'est également a notre point de vue français que ce livre offre un réel intérêt."

Two Volumes, Demy Quarto; 1000 Pages; 1400 Illustrations
Price Two Guineas net ($16.75).

An Introduction to English Church Architecture

From the Eleventh to the Sixteenth Century

By FRANCIS BOND

SOME PRESS NOTICES

Athenæum.—"These volumes form a worthy sequel to the important work on 'Gothic Architecture in England,' by the same author, published in 1905. They represent a vast amount of orderly labour, and show an astonishingly wide grasp of a great subject. It is a big undertaking; 1000 quarto pages, with 1400 illustrations. One of the pleasant features of the work is the sparing use of exceptional or technical terms, the exact meaning of which is grasped as a rule only by a professed architect. For the use of the unlearned, the first volume opens with a tersely-written glossary of terms, and this is followed by a most useful explanatory list of French words and phrases of an architectural character. But for the most part there is a breezy freshness about Mr Bond's phrases which at once rivets the attention."

Westminster Gazette.—"We know Mr Bond as a careful student, of sound scholarship, but if we had no other evidence, this 'Introduction' of his would mark him also as a writer of imagination who has not allowed the infinite detail of his subject to obscure his sight of the building. 'It is good for those who are to be introduced to mediæval church architecture,' he writes in his preface, 'to know not only how a church was built, but why it was built, who built it, who served in it, who worshipped in it, and what manner of worship was theirs—Ancient or Modern.' Already we are beginning to regard such an attitude as perfectly natural, forgetting that the text-books of the last century took no more account of the human impulse than a treatise on trigonometry takes of the private life of Euclid. . . . The book is magnificently illustrated."

Yorkshire Observer.—"Mr Bond shows, step by step, how the church varied from age to age, structure following need, so that an ancient parish church as we see it now is not a mere bit of ingenious or clumsy designing, plain or beautiful by caprice, but a living organism reflecting the lives, the faith, and indeed the material fortunes of the people who built and used it. It is in the realisation of this soul of a building more than in anything else that the difference lies between the old guide-book antiquarianism and the new archæology which Mr Bond represents. . . . If it were not so easy and lucid to read, one might compare it with Darwin's 'Origin of Species.'"

Connoisseur.—"An unrivalled record of English ecclesiastical architecture. It is difficult to speak in too high praise of the work. Mr Bond has explored his subject from end to end."

Western Mail.—"Splendidly bound and well printed, with a glossary of terms which will prove most useful to the lay reader, it is a work of the greatest value to all who are in any way interested in the construction, details, and uses of our ancient and beautiful churches."

Antiquary.—"The student or the general reader who wishes to have an intelligent grasp of principles and of their illustration and exemplification in the

Vault of Choir of Gloucester Cathedral

details of construction has here provided for him an ideal book. Mr Bond's pages are likely, however, to fascinate the expert as well as the beginner. . . . For this valuable book the author will receive the grateful thanks of students, not only those of the present time but those of many a day to come. . . . Every chapter and every section is lavishly illustrated, not at random, but by a carefully chosen set of examples closely related to the text; the wealth of illustration is so great that a full half of the thousand pages of the two volumes is occupied by pictures."

Uniform with the above Volumes of the English Church Art Series

ENGLISH CHURCH PLATE

By Rev. J. T. EVANS, M.A.

Editor of "Church Plate of Gloucestershire, Cardiganshire, Pembroke," etc.

CHURCH CHESTS, DOORS, COLLECTING AND POOR BOXES, PRESSES, ETC.

By PHILIP MAINWARING JOHNSTON

F.S.A., F.R.I.B.A.

Author of numerous Papers in the "Surrey and Sussex Archæological Collections,"
and in the "Archæological Journal."

TOMBS AND MONUMENTS IN ENGLISH CHURCHES

By F. E. HOWARD

Author of papers on "Fan Vaulting," "English Chantry Chapels,"
"Devon Churches," etc.

OXFORD UNIVERSITY PRESS